Light on the Dark Passages of Scripture

LIGHT
ON THE
DARK PASSAGES
OF SCRIPTURE

MARK GISZCZAK

Our Sunday Visitor Publishing Division
Our Sunday Visitor, Inc.
Huntington, Indiana 46750

Nihil Obstat
Msgr. Michael Heintz, Ph.D.
Censor Librorum

Imprimatur
✠ Kevin C. Rhoades
Bishop of Fort Wayne-South Bend
August 28, 2015

The *Nihil Obstat* and *Imprimatur* are official declarations that a book is free from doctrinal or moral error. It is not implied that those who have granted the *Nihil Obstat* and *Imprimatur* agree with the contents, opinions, or statements expressed.

Our Sunday Visitor Publishing Division, Our Sunday Visitor, Inc., 200 Noll Plaza, Huntington, IN 46750; 1-800-348-2440.

ISBN: 978-1-61278-803-6 (Inventory No. T1609)
eISBN: 978-1-61278-371-0
LCCN: 2015949862

Cover design: Tyler Ottinger
Cover art: Shutterstock

PRINTED IN THE UNITED STATES OF AMERICA

ENDORSEMENTS

"This is the best book I know that explains—and doesn't explain away—the truly difficult texts of Scripture. Based on solid scholarship but written in clear, crisp, contemporary language this book will help everyone to understand God's plan of progressive revelation. I can't recommend this book enough!"

Ralph Martin, S.T.D.

"We love sacred Scripture, but what about those passages that talk about polygamy, rape, war, hell, judgment, and punishments? In *Light on the Dark Passages of Scripture*, Mark Giszczak guides us through the museum of 'dark passages' and eventually leads us to the display of God's love in Christ as the answer to the human messiness of redemptive history."

Taylor Marshall, Ph.D.

CONTENTS

PART I

Confronting
a Conundrum

Chapter 1

Gut Reactions to the Old Testament God

I remember his face. My friend was outraged. He asked, "Can you envision grabbing a little boy by his curly hair and slitting his throat with a sword—*all in the name of God?*" His gestures displayed the grotesque act, and his expression revealed his anger at my obstinacy. I found myself in the awkward position of trying to defend the seemingly indefensible, the command that God gave to his people in the Old Testament to conquer the Canaanites and kill every man, woman, and child. The horror of this command and its practical consequences prompted my friend's outburst. I wanted to explain but was at a loss for words. I wanted to show him how this terrifying instruction fit into the plan of a loving, merciful God who sent his Son to die for our sins, but I couldn't formulate a convincing explanation.

You don't have to look very far in the Old Testament to find some "problems" to deal with: Why does God strike down the Egyptian firstborn? Why does God order Abraham to sacrifice his son? Why does Elijah slaughter the four hundred fifty prophets of Baal? Why does God send plagues on his people that wipe out thousands? Why does God approve the seemingly vigilante justice of "heroes" such as Phinehas, who skewered an adulterous couple with a spear? If you've spent considerable time reading the Bible, you'll have a whole laundry list of "problems." By problems, I mean those events or teachings in biblical history that don't easily line up with what we know about God from the New Testament and the teachings of the Church.

At times, the problems can prompt you to shift in your chair or feel a bit squeamish. But other times, the problems can result in a crisis of faith. In fact, many atheist writers cite the challenging passages of the Old Testament when they rail against Christian belief and practice. Not everyone demands a solution to these thorny issues, but many use them as a reason, or perhaps an excuse, to dismiss the God of the Bible as an angry, harsh, cruel power-monger. Oftentimes we are left without answers, without an adequate response to offer to those who challenge our faith because of these so-called dark passages. Yet it is crucial that we can respond well—for our own faith, for our Christian friends whose faith may be tested by the dark passages, and in a special way for non-Christians who resist the Gospel because of the Old Testament. If we can show how the dark passages comport with an ethical Christian worldview, how they reveal God, how they prepare for Christ, then perhaps we can be better witnesses for him.

Solutions Good and Bad

Unfortunately, Scriptures that make us squirm are tough to deal with. Their very darkness can lead us into overly simplistic or simply incorrect interpretations. In order to read Scripture correctly, we should be looking for what the human author and divine Author intended, how the whole fits together, and how it can be understood in the context of the Christian tradition.[1] But before we get down to the details of applying such an approach, we need to look at a few bad solutions to our problem. The bad solutions are tempting because they are easy. They avoid the hard questions, and they let us off the hook. The trouble is that they don't say what needs to be said. They don't address the atheist's deep question. They dodge the problems rather than taking them head-on.

The first bad solution is what I call the "shrug." The shrug happens when a Bible reader is happily reading along, perhaps even praying the Psalms, and comes across a line like, "Blessed is the one who seizes and smashes your children against the rock" (Ps 137:9). Rather than being startled, getting angry, or standing in awe of God's mystery, this Bible reader says to himself: "That's weird! Well, it *is* the *Old* Testament." He shrugs, moves on, and doesn't give it another thought. This easy solution is practical, but it is simply a dodge of the problem, not an explanation. It cannot survive the onslaught of hard questions from doubters. The shrug avoids the issues, but can't answer them.

> *Unfortunately, Scriptures that make us squirm are tough to deal with. Their very darkness can lead us into overly simplistic or simply incorrect interpretations.*

The second bad solution is a form of spiritualization. There is a good kind of spiritual reading, and I'll talk about that later in the book. But this bad form of spiritualization dodges the issues by reading every tough problem *only* at the spiritual level, without honoring and respecting the foundational importance of the literal sense. It says that Psalm 137:9 is about destroying the beginnings of sin by smashing temptations against the rock of Christ, *not* about smashing the babies of Babylon. This avoids, rather than solves, the problem with which this passage confronts us. St. Thomas Aquinas and other theological authorities such as the Pontifical Biblical Commission warn us that every spiritual interpretation must be founded on the literal sense.[2] We can't escape the centrality and priority of the literal sense. If we over-spiritualize the text and don't honor what the words actually convey, then we strip it of its power, steal its significance, and undercut whatever spiritual meanings we might be trying to construct.

The third bad solution originated in ancient times, but many modern people succumb to it. This solution separates the "God of the Old Testament" from the "God of the New Testament." It pits the two main parts of the Bible against each other, claiming that the two "Gods" we find in them are different. The ancient heretic Marcion proposed this idea: He and his followers actually threw out the Old Testament and used only some of the New. This also is an easy solution, a dodge, which promotes the New Testament as a trump card over the Old Testament. In this view, the Old Testament can't really reveal God to us; it just gives us a false, menacing portrait of God that doesn't tell us who he is. Now Marcion and his followers died a long time ago, but it is tempting for us to become practical Marcionites, carrying around only the New Testament, reading only the New Testament, and putting the Old Testament on the back burner as if it can't really reveal God to us.

But this "Marcionite" solution forgets that the New Testament is based on the Old, that Jesus saw himself not as abolishing the Old Testament Law and Prophets, but fulfilling them (Mt 5:17). The New Testament constantly quotes the Old, and when St. Paul refers to "Scripture"—and how it is God-breathed and useful (2 Tm 3:16)—he is referring primarily to the Old Testament, since the New Testament had not yet been compiled. Matthew, Paul, Peter, and other New Testament writers constantly quote Old Testament texts to prove their points, to show how Jesus fulfills the Old Testament. The two Testaments are inextricably linked. New Testament religion is founded upon Old Testament religion. Even if you wanted to keep the New and not the Old, you would have to cut out vast portions of the New that quote the Old. Marcion's solution can't work—again, it sidesteps the issues rather than addressing them.

The fourth bad solution gets closer to the truth, but misses the mark. This solution suggests that each time we confront a "problem" we are really confronting a misunderstanding. For example, those who embrace this view would argue that God did not really command the Israelites to kill the Canaanites; they just misinterpreted what God wanted. Or when Elijah executes the prophets of Baal, these interpreters would argue that he wasn't really doing what God wanted, but overstepping and engaging in a vicious human act, a crime of murder. The trouble with this approach is that it does not treat the Bible as divine revelation. Rather, it treats the Bible as a storybook that must constantly be supervised, judged, and reinterpreted in light of some external code of morality or justice. The external code—whether it be the New Testament or a philosophical concept of justice—places limits on God's "behavior" and forces every Old Testament conundrum through an extrinsic intellectual funnel. It prevents the Old Testament from teaching us who God is and instead places us above the text, dictating to it what God must be like and how he must act. This perspective destroys the revelatory power of the Old Testament and confines its role to showing us the acts of many people who misinterpreted God's commands. Rather than the Old Testament revealing God to us, we must reveal God to it by straightening out all of its imperfections. There must be a better way!

Finding God in the Dark

I don't want to suggest that I will be able to solve all of your Bible-reading problems, but I can promise not to dodge them. This book is really an introduction to the difficulties.[3] My aim is to give you the tools you need to not just apologetically explain—that is, defend—some challenging moments in the Bible, but to show others how even some of the darkest passages reveal God and his plan of salvation to us. For many who reject the Bible or embrace one of the "bad solutions" I've mentioned, the Bible *seems* to present a contradictory vision of God—a God of wrath and a God of mercy, the "God of the Old Testament" and the "God of the New Testament." I want to show you how these two "Gods" can be reconciled, how it is that we can fully embrace the God of justice and fully receive the God of mercy. In fact, I will argue that the tension between justice and mercy is absolutely necessary for a good understanding of God and of what he has done for us.

> *Struggling over some of the details in the problematic passages of the Bible should help us arrive at a deeper knowledge of God.*

Not only is it theologically necessary to wrestle with these issues, but it is particularly timely. A few years ago, Pope Benedict XVI mentioned "those passages in the Bible which, due to the violence and immorality they occasionally contain, prove obscure and difficult."[4] He wrote that "it would be a mistake to neglect those passages of Scripture that strike us as problematic."[5] Even he rejected the "shrug" solution! Struggling over some of the details in the problematic passages of the Bible should help us arrive at a deeper knowledge of God, of who he is and how he operates. To abandon some parts of Scripture for the sake of others is to ignore certain parts of God's revelation to us, to set aside things that he considers important enough to record for us in his Word.

While it may be tempting to give in to your gut reaction, turn the page in disgust, and avoid the hard work of thinking through the difficult problems the Bible presents to us, this book will help you dig in and stand your ground, to let the texts that have proven challenging to you become a source not of frustration but of revelation. In fact, the early Church Father St. Augustine suggests that God deliberately put difficulties in sacred Scripture *in order* for us to take the time to ponder them, meditate on them, and strive for better understanding.[6] He considers the obscurity of Scripture to be "beneficial" in this way. I hope that you will find this brief study of scriptural obscurities to be intellectually beneficial and spiritually fruitful. I envision us looking through the window of Scripture at God. Let's clean the glass so we can get a clearer glimpse!

Chapter 2

Justice vs. Mercy

American culture is bipolar when it comes to punishment. On the one hand, we hate the idea of doling out punishments. On the other, we are the most punitive nation in the world.

In 2008, when the body of a two-year-old Orlando girl was found with duct tape over her mouth in the woods near her family's home, and evidence of chloroform and human decomposition were found in the trunk of her mother's car, no one was brought to justice. Though the mother, Casey Anthony, had searched the Internet for "neck breaking" and "how to chloroform," she received nothing but a hand slap from the court. In a different case, the 1994 Menendez trial, two brothers murdered their parents with shotguns, but the original jury ended up undecided after the defense argued that the brothers had no moral responsibility for the murders because of their abusive upbringing. However, such leniency should not be surprising in a culture that doles out trophies for everyone and punishes teachers for giving failing grades to students. Yet somehow our culture not only despises but also embraces the handing out of just deserts.

Packed Prisons

While we can't stand the thought of a student failing a class, we love to put people in prison—and for a long time, too. The United States has the highest incarceration rate of any country in the world. Many states have mandatory sentencing rules that force judges to give years-long sentences for certain offenses, without wiggle room for mitigating circumstances. While most countries imprison fewer than two hundred people per one hundred thousand residents, the United States imprisons over seven hundred, more than three times as many! So we seem to like a stiff dose of justice when a person has been officially convicted of a crime, but a blanket of wishy-washy clemency for most behavior.

Part of our cultural bias might be rooted in our out-of-sight-out-of-mind mentality. Most of us don't visit the local courthouse (let alone prison!) to watch justice being dispensed. Such an experience might make us feel uneasy when we watch the consequences of a person's actions tear his or her life apart. If other people, whom we pay and to whom we give strict rules, take care of the decisions and actions involved in criminal justice, then we don't have to worry about it. We can go about our business and keep "troublemakers" out of view. If we were tasked with the job of the prosecutor, judge, or jury, our feelings might be different. Jury service, which we usually see as an arduous annoyance, is one of the few times we actually get to participate in the process. It might even modify our perspective.

Abstract rules such as mandatory sentencing requirements or laws that prohibit certain behaviors are comforting because they are detached from the actual human beings whose lives will be affected. Once we get our hands dirty in the execution of justice, it's hard to be so coldly rational. So we vacillate between justice and mercy. We might incarcerate almost one percent of our citizens, but at least we pay their cable TV bills.[7] Mercy is easier to dispense because it seems to require nothing of us, but we'll see that this is not really the case.

The problem with the American approach to punishment is that it doesn't work. The prison system might punish a person for criminal behavior, but, generally, it doesn't *change* people. Politicians talk about the issue of "repeat offenders," recidivism, and the lack of "rehabilitation." There's something missing in our approach to justice and mercy. We like to exact serious penalties, and yet those exactions don't have the results we hope for. Putting someone in one of our prisons for years is no guarantee that he or she will be a new person upon release.

> *The problem with the American approach to punishment is that it doesn't work. The prison system might punish a person for criminal behavior, but, generally, it doesn't change people.*

Our hearts might lean toward mercy, toward being soft and gentle, toward kid-glove treatment. Whether it be grade inflation, trophies for everyone, or an overly comfortable prison environment, we are somewhat allergic to punishment. I've wondered why this might be the case, and I think part of it is that when we look inside our own hearts, we realize that we too deserve punishment for our own sins and failings. To be overly eager in handing out judgment could backfire. We ourselves could fall victim to the punitive policies that we create.

The Need for Punishment

However, sometimes judgment must fall quickly and harshly. The most dramatic example from our culture is the Nuremberg trials. After the horrors of the Holocaust and German aggression, the Allied powers which won World War II sat down to the messy business of holding those responsible to account. Twenty-four Nazi leaders were tried, and most were convicted and punished. Fifteen years later, one of the leading Nazis responsible for the Holocaust, Adolf Eichmann, was captured in Argentina by a team of Israeli agents and brought back to Israel for a publicly televised trial. While no amount of trials could undo the damage wrought by the Third Reich, the public could feel in the trials a great sense of relief at the fact that justice was being served. Evil acts and serious wrongdoing were being examined in the light of day and responded to with stringent punishment. Swift and certain justice was handed down, and the malevolent Nazi project was being brought to an appropriately ignominious close.

While we might want to speculate about the details of our origins or the path of human evolution, there is no doubt that we human beings are stained by sin. The tale of Adam and Eve conveys this fact in storybook language, but all we need to do is look inside our own hearts to know that its message is true. No amount of paleontological digging or DNA sequencing will prove otherwise. We could not handle the gift of our own existence.

While we might not like dealing with the trouble of punishment on a daily basis, we actually find solace in the punishment of wrongdoers when it comes to dramatic cases. Serious wrongs deserve serious righting, and that means serious punishment. Violent acts, especially against the vulnerable, justly prompt moral outrage, and moral outrage can only be satisfied by just punishment. Tragically, we can't undo the evils caused by evildoers, but at least we can hold perpetrators to account. Their freedom can be taken away by prison, and in extreme cases—which are, in Pope St. John Paul II's words, "very rare, if not practically nonexistent"—their lives can be taken away by capital punishment.[8] While we might like to be lenient, the Nuremberg trials illustrate the moral necessity of justice and punishment. We cannot be lenient forever.

Ancient Sins

Now while our intuition can clue us in to the importance of dealing out punishment to mass murderers or child abusers, the first injustice and the first punishment in human history demands more subtle investigation. Adam and Eve found themselves as God's first human children, enjoying the pleasures of the Garden of Eden and communion with God and one another. But when the serpent introduces discord into the Garden with his smooth and deliciously deceptive words, the couple falls from grace. God had given them only one prohibition—not to eat from the Tree of Knowledge of Good and Evil—and that is the exact point on which the serpent tempts them, presenting the false hope of becoming equal with God by eating the fruit. Adam and Eve simply violate God's simple command and eat the fruit. Immediately, their mistake is apparent to them: their eyes were opened (Gn 3:7). While the nature of their error is shrouded in the symbolic language of Genesis, they find themselves truly separated from God by their own error: the original sin. Their harmony with God, their moral integrity, even their loving unity with each other were brought crashing down by their sin. Original justice devolves into original sin. Original harmony dissolves into original discord. Their disobedience impacts all humanity for all time, leaving us with a broken world, fallen away from God and in need of redemption. While we might want to speculate about the details of our origins or the path of human evolution, there is no doubt that we human beings are stained by sin. The tale of Adam and Eve conveys this fact in storybook language, but all we need to do is look inside our own hearts to know that its message is true. No amount of paleontological digging or DNA sequencing will prove otherwise. We could not handle the gift of our own existence.

God does not ignore the original sin but responds to it with justice, and yes, with punishment. God confronts Adam and Eve, asking, "What is this you have done?" (Gn 3:13). It is a question that expresses moral outrage,[9] like our, "What were you thinking?" Adam famously passes the buck to Eve, and she passes it to the serpent. No one wants to take responsibility. That is exactly why punishment must exist, to enforce moral responsibility. If an adult abuses a child, a court might not be able to restore emotional and psychological health to the child, but at least it can punish the adult offender for abdicating his or her responsibility to protect rather than exploit youths. When God responds to the serpent and Adam and Eve, he hands a curse to each—that is, a punishment for violating his law, for disrupting the order of creation, for bringing discord into the harmonious world he created (Gn 3:14-19). These curses, or punishments, are morally necessary to right the wrong done in the Garden. Pain in childbirth, toilsome work, and death come upon humanity at this moment. St. Paul teaches, "the wages of sin is death" (Rom 6:23), and Adam and Eve, by virtue of their sin, are paid the wage of death. In fact, all human beings inherit the consequences of their original sin.[10] Death was not part of God's original plan. We were supposed to be "immune" from it, but the original sin brought the consequence of death for all of us.[11]

Punishment and Redemption

Even in the context of doling out the punishment curses, God sneaks in a redemptive note. He mentions the offspring of the woman who will be an enemy of the serpent and eventually "crush" the serpent's head (Gn 3:15). While the serpent had provoked Adam and Eve to fall away from God in the Garden, justice will come full circle eventually. At the moment of the Fall, the ominous consequences of the first sin loomed large, yet God chose to promise a change, a way to undo the consequences, to right the wrong of sin. The offspring he mentions points to Christ, the one who will come to break the power of sin and release those enslaved to it into the freedom of God's children.

What we can deduce from the Fall and the moral discord between God and man which it introduces is this: suffering, punishment, and God's just judgment are rooted in original sin, in humanity's fall from grace brought about by our own actions, our own choice against God. Adam and Eve started the ball rolling. The wonderful harmony they enjoyed with God was not only damaged, but smashed to pieces by their violation of his simple command. They deliberately broke their relationship with God, and so God meted out punishment to them. The moral consequences of evil actions lead to suffering and harm. God's judgment with its attendant punishments addresses evil action and aims to right the wrongs humanity brings forth. Yet in an odd way, just punishment is a kind of mercy, since punishment is meant to lead to conversion, reformation, moral transformation. Punishment is not only punitive but instructive.

We were supposed to be "immune" from it, but the original sin brought the consequence of death for all of us.

There is always a tension between justice and mercy. God is a just God, but he is also merciful. In the end, "mercy triumphs over judgment" (Jas 2:13), but that doesn't mean that judgment is nonsensical or unnecessary. In fact, in that same verse James says that "judgment is without mercy to one who has shown no mercy." Evil deeds ought to be repaid justly with fitting punishments. Again, this is why we hesitate to hand out punishments, because inside we realize our own moral failings and that we too deserve punishment. But punishment is only part of the story. Just punishment is fitting, yet incomplete. It appropriately responds to evil action, but it does not solve it or redeem it. Something more is needed. Long prison terms do not necessarily rehabilitate a prisoner. In fact, a long prison term could incline a person to repeat offense. A recent study showed that three-quarters of released prisoners were arrested again within five years of release.[12] While punishment is just, it does not necessarily bring the moral transformation necessary to live a flourishing human life.

This tension between mercy and justice, and the need for redemption, reveal certain dynamics of God's relationship with humanity. Our evil acts demand a just response from God, a response that includes punishment. But as sinners, we stand in need of God's mercy. Many of our sufferings, like death, originate from God's just punishment, yet he reaches out to heal us in his mercy. The tensions we see in the Bible between justice and mercy stem from our troubled relationship with him; sometimes we act in loving obedience, and sometimes we rebel. God's justice appropriately punishes wrongdoing, but his mercy and redemption invite us to something even greater than satisfying the demands of justice.

Chapter 3

God the Just Judge

God sits on a throne. The Bible pictures him this way multiple times—in the Psalms, Isaiah, Revelation, even the Gospels.[13] Thrones conjure images of kingship in our minds, but most of us know more about kings from fairy-tale picture books than from personal experience. Our inner child says that a king wears a crown and a red robe with ermine lining. He has big gold rings and feasts sumptuously every day. We might even think he's like a president, handing down orders and appointing people to important positions. But kingship is different from presidency, even in the case of JFK's "Camelot." In theory, the king holds all power. In the American system, power is divided into the legislative, executive, and judicial branches. However, in an absolute monarchy, all power is contained in one person. The king is legislator, executive, and judge.

We see the judicial role of the ancient Israelite king in the story about Solomon judging between two women who both claim the same baby as their own (1 Kgs 3:16-28).[14] They bring their case before Solomon, and he famously offers to have the baby sliced in half and divided between the women. The true mother reacts with horror and offers to give the baby to the other woman. Solomon thus reveals who the true mother is and restores the baby to her. The story is meant to demonstrate Solomon's wisdom, but it also shows something else—that the king was not only the chief executive, but he was the chief judge of the system of justice. Ideally, a complex or hard-fought case could eventually be appealed from a local official to the king himself. Now, exactly how efficiently or perfectly this system of appeal worked is not our concern here.[15] The point is that the king operated as a judge, and the throne is not just a symbol of executive power or regal pomp, but a symbol for the king's judicial authority.

At the end of time, after God has completed all of his judicial work, we won't be able to say, "That's not fair!" about anything in the universe.

In our culture, the bench on which the judge sits symbolizes his authority. We often hear talk of "the bench" as in when a judge invites lawyers to "approach the bench" or when newspapers discuss new judicial appointments. (The bar, on the other hand, divides the area where the lawyers, jury, and parties to the case sit from the seats for the general public.) Nowadays, most judges sit on a nice leather office chair, rather than a stiff bench, but the point is that the place where the judge sits stands for the judge's power. In the Bible, God's throne indicates his kingly judicial authority, his power as the final arbitrator of all cases.

Hope in Judgment

Now this concept of God as the final judge of all things can prompt either hope or despair. On earth, many cases are left unsolved, many injustices are never righted, many times justice is left unserved or incompletely served. But if, ultimately, the one being in (or above) the universe with total power also will act as a perfect judge, we have hope that all of the injustices in our world will someday be "put to rights." And all of the incomplete ministrations of human, earthly justice will be brought to completion in God's eternal, perfect justice. At the end of time, after God has completed all of his judicial work, we won't be able to say, "That's not fair!" about anything in the universe. This is a great hope! However, the despair I mentioned might jump up in our hearts if we find ourselves on the wrong side of God's ultimate justice. If we have hidden sins, secret crimes, everything we have done will eventually come to light before the all-knowing God, and we'll be judged not according to how people saw us, but according to who we really are and what we have really done.[16] That can be kind of scary, but there is no reason to despair since God offers us a possibility of redemption and hope, but more on that later.

Even the Caesar of the Roman Empire would judge cases. Emperor Claudius was famous for spending much of his time adjudicating cases personally.[17] Even St. Paul, when he is on trial in the book of Acts (25:11), appeals his case to Caesar. Tradition has it that Nero initially dismissed his case,[18] but later, when Paul was arrested again, the emperor had him executed.[19] Thus even Caesar, as the monarch of a political system switching from democracy to dictatorship, acted with judicial authority. He was not only the supreme executive of Rome, but the supreme judge.

The beauty of this divine justice is that it is perfect. No stone will be left unturned. No evidence will be left out. No one will walk away complaining about an unjust verdict or a biased judge.

Human judges like Caesar or Solomon must always base their decisions on the testimony of witnesses, the evidence of objects and documents, and their own horse-sense wisdom. This last element is often the most important. Robots wouldn't make very good judges since they can't read people, rely on experience, or develop shrewd judgment the same way people can. Human justice is not mechanistic but always has the X factor of human subjectivity. For example, a judge can decide that leniency is to be pursued in a case where the defendant has committed her first crime and has children to care for, but strictness is the order of the day when the defendant has a long rap sheet and needs to be taught a lesson.

Divine justice is different. Since God is all-knowing he does not need to rely on the faulty memories of human witnesses or the difficult-to-decipher physical evidence. Rather, he can know absolutely what a person has done and what their intentions were. His wisdom is complete. His judgment is always on target. He says, "I know your works" (Rv 2:2), and the Bible also teaches that "before him no creature is hidden" (Heb 4:13). Again, this omniscience can be either frightening or relieving. While we talk about having to "give an account" to God, his all-seeing knowledge does not need our help. He will know what we're going to say before it comes out of our mouth. The beauty of this divine justice is that it is perfect. No stone will be left unturned. No evidence will be left out. No one will walk away complaining about an unjust verdict or a biased judge. Instead, when we walk away from the divine "bench" or throne, we will all be satisfied with the result.

King David and Divine Justice

One biblical example of divine justice will help us think through the judicial power behind God's throne: the story of David. David was the first great king of Israel. He firmly established the throne, fought off Israel's enemies and was "a man after God's own heart" (see 1 Sm 13:14). He was brave and just, holy and devout. It seemed that everything in his life was going right; he was destined to be a hero for God's people! Yet even in the best of persons, sometimes things go awry. One year, during his reign as king, David sits out the battle season (2 Sm 11). Instead of going out with his courageous army, he stays at home at his palace. Then as he strolls along the roof of his palace, which overlooks the regular homes below, he notices a lovely naked woman bathing in her backyard. Desire consumes him. He acts before he thinks. He summons her and sleeps with her. He abuses his kingly authority, his appointment by God, the trust placed in him as king, by taking advantage of a woman with no royal status or political importance. Her husband was a soldier, out to battle with David's army (absent David). When the woman, Bathsheba, tells David that she has become pregnant by him, he is horrified and tries to cover his tracks.

He invites Bathsheba's husband, Uriah, back from the battlefront. He asks him questions about the battle and suggests he go home and pay a visit to his wife. But Uriah can't stand the thought of going home when his comrades are camping out and fighting a battle, so he sleeps in the barracks at the palace. When David invites him back and plies him with wine, Uriah still refuses to go home. David feels backed into a corner—his sin will be a public scandal if there is no denying the child is his—so he sends Uriah back to the battlefront. Devilishly, he sends a sealed message with Uriah to the commander at the front. The message is Uriah's death warrant: it asks the commander to put Uriah's unit in an untenable position in the battle and then draw back so that Uriah will be killed. In one fell swoop, David breaks a bunch of the Ten Commandments: he covets his neighbor's wife, steals her, commits adultery, lies about his actions, murders, and dishonors God. Even though previously he had been so faithful to God, his sins are egregious. They demand justice. They require punishment.

However, being the king and chief judge has its perks. It is easy to be above the law. No one has judicial power over you. David sits on his royal throne untouched, that is, until God intervenes. The Lord sends Nathan the prophet to confront David.

Even though Nathan is a prophet of God, he must watch his steps before the king, especially one who has just murdered an innocent servant. Because of this, Nathan comes before David and simply tells a story. The story goes something like this: There was a rich man and a poor man. The rich man had a big house, lots of money, and lots of sheep and goats. The poor man had a little house and just one little lamb that he loved so dearly that it slept in his bed every night as a beloved pet. One day, the rich man had an out-of-town visitor, and he wanted to lay a big feast before him. But instead of using one of his own sheep, he went next door to the poor man's house, took away the beloved pet lamb, and slaughtered it to feed to his guest. This vicious thief's dinner roused David's ire, and he cried out, "As the LORD lives, the man who has done this deserves to die!" (2 Sm 12:5). With powerful poetic irony, David thus calls down a curse upon himself. To add icing on the cake and seal David's guilt, Nathan points his finger at David and says, "You are the man!" (2 Sm 12:7).

I can imagine David's face turning white as a sheet as the full realization of what has just happened strikes him. "If Nathan knows, everyone knows. I just cursed the man in the name of the Lord, but *I am the man!*" The judgment has been pronounced. David realizes that his toxic sins would be justly punished by death. The prophet lists David's sins in detail and announces his punishment, yet Nathan actually has some good news: "you shall not die." But it is worth looking in detail at what the punishment will be:

> "Now therefore the sword shall never depart from your house, because you have despised me, and have taken the wife of Uriah the Hittite to be your wife. Thus says the LORD, 'Behold, I will raise up evil against you out of your own house; and I will take your wives before your eyes, and give them to your neighbor, and he shall lie with your wives in the sight of this sun. For you did it secretly; but I will do this thing before all Israel, and before the sun.'" David said to Nathan, "I have sinned against the LORD." And Nathan said to David, "The LORD also has put away your sin; you shall not die. Nevertheless, because by this deed you have utterly scorned the LORD, the child that is born to you shall die." (2 Sm 12:10-14)

In the drama of the story, David fasts and prays for the life of the baby born from the adulterous union, but it eventually dies of illness. After the baby's death, David responds: "Why should I fast? Can I bring him back again? I shall go to him, but he will not return to me" (2 Sm 12:23).

The Punishment of David

Interestingly, the Lord forgives David but still punishes him. Many preachers use a baseball analogy to explain this one. If you're in the backyard and hit a ball through your neighbor's window, the neighbor might forgive you, but someone still needs to pay for the window. Here, the same principle is in play. David has broken his covenant with the Lord, "despised" him by his sinful actions. His violation of Bathsheba, his murder of Uriah, and his duplicity all need to be addressed and punished even though the Lord "has put away" his sin. The Lord does not inflict the death penalty on David but does punish him. Now David's punishment bears some parsing. To me, it looks as if we actually have three distinct punishments: (1) the "sword" will afflict his descendants; (2) his wives will be publicly ravished by his "neighbor"; (3) the baby Bathsheba bore him will die. The weird thing about these punishments from a modern perspective is that none of them afflict David as an individual. Nothing touches him bodily, so we might think: "That's unfair! All these other people get punished for David's personal sin. How about David? Why doesn't he get sick and die?" However, this observation overlooks the interpersonal connectedness of the ancient world and of traditional cultures today.

In these cultures, children and descendants are of paramount importance. They are the future. To harm my children, to afflict them in any way does more damage to me than to harm my body. Even in modern cultures, to threaten someone's children is to threaten him or her. One needs only to think of action movies in which a child is held for ransom or a spy's children are kidnapped in order to force an adult to fork over cash or otherwise capitulate. But in David's case, the Lord's "sword" threat is especially ominous. Just a few chapters earlier, the Lord had promised that David's descendants would have an everlasting throne, but now they will have an everlasting sword. This raises a question: Does God want David to be afflicted? I think the answer is no, but David and his descendants will be afflicted as the due punishment, the logical outworking, even the natural consequence of David's sin. In the same way that a person's vices—whether smoking, drinking, drug use, *et cetera*—can harm his or her children, David's sins will harm his family tree in a grievous way. In fact, as we read through the rest of Samuel and Kings, we see that indeed the sword does not leave David's royal heirs alone.

David's punishment bears some parsing. To me, it looks like we actually have three distinct punishments: (1) the "sword" will afflict his descendants; (2) his wives will be publicly ravished by his "neighbor"; (3) the baby Bathsheba bore him will die.

David's traditional ancient culture included a powerful honor/shame system. In such a culture, to be able to live with honor is more important than to live at all. If a rival publicly humiliates David by ravishing his wives on the palace rooftop, the shame would be unbearable. Indeed, later in his reign, David is forced to flee from Jerusalem when one of his sons usurps the throne. Absalom's coup is supported by the majority of the people, and as part of his takeover, Absalom publicly goes into a tent to sleep with the ten concubines David had left in the palace when he fled (2 Sm 15:16 and 16:22). On the one hand, Absalom's despicable act would be part of any throne takeover in a kingdom where the king kept a harem—the possession of the king's wives and concubines would signify kingship, and the king's marriages represented diplomatic alliances—so it is a specifically political act, a royal marriage to the former king's consorts. Similarly, David had taken Saul's wives when he became king (2 Sm 12:8). On the other hand, we can see in Absalom's political act a fulfillment of Nathan's prediction of divine punishment. Indeed, at the instigation of Bathsheba's grandfather, Ahithophel, David's courtesans are publicly ravished on the same roof from which he first lusted after Bathsheba.[20] The repugnance and poetic justice of it are startling, but the punishment fits the crime. David stole Uriah's wife, and now his concubines are stolen from him. While it is horrifying to our sensibilities, these women would have been subject to whichever claimant to the throne controlled the palace. For all they knew, Absalom would be their king and husband for the rest of their lives. The punishment, the embarrassment, and the shame fall on David. The women themselves are not punished, but transferred from one claimant to another, albeit unjustly.[21] In fact, when David returns, he sets these concubines aside and does not have relations with them again (2 Sm 20:3).

Last, the baby who is the result of David's union with Bathsheba is clearly not at fault. Yet his father's sin brings death upon him. Here, our gut jumps up to say: "Hey! It's not the baby's fault. Why punish the baby?" But primarily, David is being punished for his sin. He will not get to enjoy this child, for the child is taken away. If death were the end of the story, this would have an unbearable finality to it, yet notice David's words about the child: "I shall go to him, but he will not return to me" (2 Sm 12:23). David recognizes that in death he will meet his child. While the child suffers death as a result of his father's sin, in the ultimate course of God's justice and mercy, death is not the end.

David's story teaches us a few things about God. God reigns not just as an executive, but as a judge. He sees all that we do and justly determines what we deserve. Sadly, the con-

sequences of our sins and offenses against God are not confined to us as individuals. We are all connected for good or for
ill. When we act rightly, love others, and obey God's law, our
lives are blessings to our family and friends, but when we do
evil and break God's commandments, our lives become the
opposite. Our sins and failings bring down evil consequences
on those around us, including our children. David's sin harms
not only himself, but his whole family tree. Even though God
"puts away" his sin, in justice the punishment must be admin-
istered. David, his family, and his nation suffer because of his
evil choices. Punishment is not silly or random; rather it restores the order of justice. God teaches us that punishment reveals something about who we are, about who he is, and about
how the universe works. In fact, we'll see that God's justice
teaches us by design. He intends to reveal himself through his
intervention in human history.

Chapter 4

God the Teacher

If I woke you up by shining a flashlight in your eyes, you probably wouldn't thank me. If I tried to teach you differential calculus before you knew how to add and subtract, we probably wouldn't get very far. If I chose to teach you a foreign language only by talking quickly in complex sentences in that language, you probably wouldn't pick it up. Underlying these problems is an important principle: good teaching follows good order. You have to learn one thing before you can learn another. Start with the basics and proceed to more complex ideas. Turn the light up slowly.

Since he's a teacher, God knows this principle. In fact, as the only omniscient being, he's the best teacher. But if you think about what it would be like to be an infinite being trying to communicate with limited, finite, problematic beings like us, you can see that there's a bit of a gap. Just imagine Albert Einstein trying to teach his theory of relativity to kindergarteners. For anything to stick, God has to teach us according to our capacity—and our capacity is *very* limited compared with his. Fortunately, God is not a disconnected college professor type. He's not a mere subject-matter expert with quirky habits and lousy social skills; he's perfect in every way. So he makes for a great expert *and* a great teacher, the best combination.

Gradualism

The central idea in God's pedagogy is gradualism. The *Catechism of the Catholic Church* teaches, "The divine plan of Revelation...involves a specific divine pedagogy: God communicates himself to man gradually."[22] This may seem like a no-brainer—that education has to happen in stages—but when we reflect on the history of salvation, sometimes we would prefer for there to be no stages at all. Why didn't Jesus come right after the Fall? Why did God put the Tree in the Garden of Eden in the first place? How come he let his people languish in sin and suffering for so long before he put the final stage of his rescue plan into effect? These questions all get at the nature of God's teaching, his pedagogy. The Old Testament displays the divine pedagogy in action. God slowly, over the course of time, reveals more and more of who he is to humanity.

The central idea in God's pedagogy is gradualism.

A lot of the Old Testament stories that perplex us as "dark" passages can be understood through the principle of the divine pedagogy. For example, the ten plagues, which the Lord sends against Pharaoh and the Egyptians, show his teaching style. The Exodus story is very familiar to us—God sends his servant Moses to Pharaoh to ask that the enslaved people of Israel be freed for a few days to go into the desert and worship the Lord (Ex 5:1). It is a simple enough request, but Pharaoh resists God and refuses to allow the people freedom to worship. In order to convince Pharaoh, the Lord sends a series of plagues against him and the Egyptians (Ex 7–12). The plagues start out as mere demonstrations: water turning to blood, annoying frogs. But as Pharaoh refuses after each plague to let the people of Israel go, the plagues get more and more severe. The livestock die, the people are afflicted with boils, and eventually, when Pharaoh persists in his obstinate refusal, the Lord sends the angel of death to wipe out the firstborn of Egypt. While there are a lot of interesting questions to probe in this story, the main point I want to focus on is that God is *gradually* punishing Pharaoh for his resistance. He does not send the angel of death right away, but slowly turns up the heat as Pharaoh refuses again and again to let the people of Israel go and worship.

Jesus, in the course of his own three-year ministry, uses the same method that the Holy Trinity uses throughout the Bible: teach gradually.

Lessons in Order

We see a similar teaching method in the life of Jesus. He doesn't jump up right away as a baby and tell everyone, "I am the light of the world!" Instead, he waits until he is thirty years old to initiate his ministry, and even then he teaches much of the time in shrouded, mysterious parables. St. John Paul II spoke of this aspect of Jesus' teaching:

> In his preaching to the crowds he used parables to communicate his teaching in a way that suited the intelligence of his listeners. In teaching his disciples he proceeded gradually, taking into account the difficulty they had in understanding. So it was only in the second part of his public life that he expressly announced his sorrowful way and only at the end did he openly declare his identity not only as the Messiah, but as the "Son of God." We note also that, in his most detailed dialogues, he communicated his revelation by answering the questions of his listeners and using language their mentality easily understood.[23]

Jesus, in the course of his own three-year ministry, uses the same method that the Holy Trinity uses throughout the Bible: teach gradually. Just like any good teacher, God communicates truths in a particular, designed order. We're not ready to hear about a Savior until we know we need saving. We're not ready to hear about repentance until we know we've broken God's law. We're not ready to hear about God's law until we know that there is a God and that he has authority over our lives.

As human teachers and learners, it is easy for us to miss steps along the way, to forget to present the truth in the proper order, but God knows the right way to do it. We might think that things would always proceed from easy to hard, or from less severe to more severe. In some ways this is true, but in others it is backward. What I mean is that, early on in the biblical story, God teaches simple lessons in simple ways. As salvation history proceeds, he teaches more and more difficult lessons in ways that are harder to understand. So, for example, to tell Adam and Eve not to eat from the Tree of the Knowledge of Good and Evil is a very simple lesson, but for Jesus to teach the apostles that they will be persecuted and need to remain faithful under torture and even death is a much harder and more complex lesson. We can grasp the meaning of these lessons by taking into account what Vatican II calls the "customary and characteristic styles of feeling, speaking and narrating which prevailed at the time."[24] The infinite God, in his effort to teach finite beings, simplifies his message to be able to reach us within the limitations of our cultural circumstances. In the ancient world, this meant teaching people who lived in a relatively primitive culture. When we see biblical laws dealing with animal sacrifices, ox-goring, ritual purity, eating blood, taking vows, leprosy, and child sacrifice, we can get a sense for the kind of culture they lived in. Life was harsher, shorter, and involved a lot of messy things. War was frequent and involved personal combat with bronze swords, spears, and bare hands. Infant mortality was normal. Plagues and famines were common. Laws were simple because life was brutal.

Preachers often talk about how reading the New Testament is like reading someone else's mail, but reading the Old Testament is like reading someone else's storybook, prayer book, law book, and prophecy book. It is not easy to read because of the vast change in cultural circumstances from Old Testament times to our own. Imagine trying to explain how to use an iPhone to an ancient Israelite. Then imagine him explaining to you how his family and clan relationships work. It's complicated. God enters into human history, but he does it on the sly. He knows our limits, our sins, the smallness of our perspectives, and he works with that. We often talk about "meeting people where they are at." God does that. He knew where the ancients were and brought them closer to himself one step at a time.

The Law of Moses

St. Paul talks about how the Old Testament law of God, the law of Moses, was like a "schoolmaster to bring us unto Christ" (Gal 3:24. Sometimes the King James puts it best!). The Greek word he uses, *paidagogos*, could be translated as tutor, teacher, pedagogue, or even as a household slave who would bring a boy to and from school. The point is that the law of Moses plays a part in our moral education. It was the "text" of the divine pedagogy. The *Catechism* itself gets at this point: "This divine pedagogy appears especially in the gift of the Law. God gave the letter of the Law as a 'pedagogue' to lead his people towards Christ."[25] The law of Moses, which has 613 commandments all told, was not meant to be God's final revelation to his people or definitive for all time. Instead, the Old Testament law is a provisional, teaching measure. It sets the stage for what follows, but it is not the conclusion of the story.

The temporary quality of Old Testament law can make it a bit confusing to interpret. Part of it we as Catholics embrace, but part of it we don't. For example, we still forbid murder (Ex 20:13), but we don't forbid wearing a garment of mixed materials (Dt 22:11). What's the rationale behind that? How come some of the law still applies—like the Ten Commandments—but some does not?

St. Thomas Aquinas can help us here. He breaks down the Old Testament laws into three categories: moral, ritual, and judicial.[26] Moral law has do with universal principles of right and wrong. Ritual or ceremonial law has to do with symbolic, religious cleanness and uncleanness in Old Testament religion. Judicial or civil law involves the structures for the administration of the law in the Old Testament. Remember that the law of Moses foresees not just a religion, but a state religion, even a theocracy. So certain features of that system don't make sense in a non-theocratic government system. Aquinas teaches that the ritual and judicial laws have been abrogated, but that the moral law still holds. So we *can* eat bacon, but we can't eat our neighbor. This three-way division of the old law is helpful, but then the interpretive trouble comes down to figuring out which of those 613 commandments fall in which category. Beyond that, we also have to ask what is the pedagogic purpose of laws that would eventually be eliminated.

The law of Moses, which has 613 command-ments all told, was not meant to be God's final revelation to his people or definitive for all time.

If we don't make these distinctions, we can fall into problematic views—becoming either libertine (thinking that no laws apply to our behavior) or wannabe Jews (where we try to observe the ritual laws of the Old Testament without actually being Jewish). Because we don't have space to sort through every law, let's focus on the overall teaching purpose of the "schoolmaster" law. What is it that the law of Moses, especially the ritual laws which we no longer observe, teaches us about living for God? The ritual laws of the Old Testament cover the minute details of life. They show us that living for God permeates every aspect of our daily lives. Every choice we make brings us closer to him or pushes him farther away. The ancient ritual system of cleanness and uncleanness we find in the

Old Testament has some similarities with the other religious systems of the ancient world, some measures directed toward health and hygiene (such as the rules about leprosy and mold spores), but the point of it all is to direct our gaze to God and show us our need for him. Many things could make a person unclean, and animal sacrifices were only partially helpful in helping a person attain ritual purity. This temporary law was a powerful teaching tool that God the Teacher uses to reveal to us our own impurity, inadequacy, and fundamental need for him to purify and cleanse us. It is one step in God's pedagogical program to instruct us about who he really is.

This means that when we read the Old Testament, we have to be conscious of the gradualism of it all. The theology of Abraham is far more advanced than that of Adam, but the theology of Isaiah is far beyond even the theology of Moses. As time goes on and God reveals more and more of himself to his people, the picture fills out. Yet it is not until Jesus comes that the fullness of revelation is realized. The *Catechism* states: "Christ, the Son of God made man, is the Father's one, perfect and unsurpassable Word. In him he has said everything; there will be no other word than this one."[27] He is the high point and the final point of divine revelation. He is the last lesson of the divine pedagogy.

Chapter 5

God the Savior

Thinking of God as a judge in a black robe and powdered wig looking down on the accused with a somber scowl and issuing his judgment in stentorian tone doesn't exactly give us the warm fuzzies. Even the awesome majesty of God on display in thunder and lightning at Mount Sinai might not make us feel comfortable. A "nice" God who conforms to our ideas and experience—dare I say, even our culture—is what we'd prefer, at least at first. But how would it be to have a God who didn't have anything to teach us? If we already knew everything we needed to and he simply helped us along our merry way, but couldn't actually *guide* us, what would we do? In addition, we tend to like the passages that talk about God as the one who "secures justice for the oppressed," who rescues the lowly and vindicates the righteous. If he were always "nice" and never fierce, how could he rescue anyone from powerful oppressors?

When some of the first apostles were evangelizing, they were arrested and charged with "turning the world upside down" (see Acts 17:6). God turns the ways of the world on their head. He is the great equalizer, the force that establishes justice firmly at the end of the day. The justice of God can be fierce, but it also can bring healing, redemption, even salvation. The trouble for our minds is holding these two characteristics in tension. We like the beautiful Garden of Eden, but it stings a bit when God kicks Adam and Eve out of it. We like justice for the oppressed, but tremble a little when the master boots wedding guests "into the outer darkness where men will weep and gnash their teeth." It might help for us to keep in mind that the execution of justice is actually an act of saving. When a murderer is sentenced for his crime, the judge "saves" the memory of the murdered person. When a judge orders a thief to pay restitution to his victims, those persons are made whole.

Justice—Harsh or Beautiful?

Justice is harsh because it seeks to undo the cruel evils of crime. Evil criminal acts are truly harsh, and justice responds by attempting as best as possible to reverse the evil effects of a crime. Sadly, in many if not most cases of earthly justice, the wrong is never truly undone. A judge cannot bring a murder victim back to life or take away the horrible experiences of an abuse victim. A judge is limited to handing down jail sentences, community service, and, on rare occasions, the death penalty (about which recent popes have expressed strong reservation[28]). Each act of sentencing, of punishment, is an attempt to restore the order of justice, to put things back the way they were before the crime was committed. This function of just punishment is beautiful and restorative. It at least tries to do what cannot completely be done: to bring salvation. However, God's acts of justice surpass earthly justice.

> *This rescue plan had multiple stages that reveal different dimensions of God's character, but, most importantly, the rescue plan shows that God the Savior and God the Judge are one and the same.*

God in fact is perfectly just, the measuring stick against which all judges can be measured. His justice does not suffer from the incompleteness that earthly justice does. But his dispensing of justice is conditioned by our circumstances—that is, we get to receive his acts of justice from his eternity

into our time-bound existence. We can be confident that in
the end he will bring all things together in his perfect justice,
but in the meantime many injustices persist. This situation has
its upside, in that God provides time for the wicked (us) to repent and so obtain salvation. Justice is about salvation, about
putting things back the way they were supposed to be, about
caring for the fatherless and the widow, about turning unjust
systems on their heads and saving "all the oppressed of the
earth" (Ps 76:9). The time between now and the final judgment
gives us an opportunity to turn to God and become a recipient
of his mercy through repentance rather than a target for his
judgment through obstinacy.

God's Rescue Plan

But God knew that we were stubborn. That's why he didn't sit
on his hands in heaven and wait for us to fail. As soon as we
dropped the ball (or the apple), he initiated a rescue plan that
would bring us back to himself and get the real order of justice
firmly established for all time. This rescue plan had multiple
stages that reveal different dimensions of God's character, but
most importantly, the rescue plan shows that God the Savior
and God the Judge are one and the same.

    After the darkness of the Fall, God could have justly
condemned humanity for breaking his law. However, he instead decided to try to save us. Even as he responds to Adam
and Eve's disobedience, he includes a note of hope when he
says to the serpent that he "will put enmity between you and
the woman, and between your offspring and hers; he will strike
your head, and you will strike his heel" (Gn 3:15, NRSV). This
might seem like a mere allusion to the fact that human feet
can stomp on ground-bound serpent heads, but many Christian interpreters have seen something far deeper: a promise
of a savior. Theologians refer to this passage as the *protoevan-
gelium*, the first gospel. Yet even after this initial announce-

ment and the punishments that accompanied it, humanity fell
back into sin and rebellion against God. He then brings upon
the world a fearsome punishment: the Great Flood. However,
even in the midst of such a terrifying judgment, his rescue
mission moves forward in the hands of his faithful shipwright,
Noah. God demonstrates his justice toward humanity through
punishment, and he demonstrates his saving love for humanity through Noah.

As we saw above, justice itself has a salvific component:
rescuing those who have suffered under injustice. But God's
justice *and* his mercy are about bringing salvation. Through
his interventions in human history, the Lord demonstrates
that he is not merely a judge, but simultaneously a judge and a
savior. He promises a savior to Adam and Eve; then he rescues
Noah's family from the Flood. Generations later, after memory
of Noah's covenant with God has faded, the Lord launches his
special rescue mission by calling Abraham out of Ur into the
Promised Land of Canaan. The Lord asks Abraham to move
not because Ur is a bad place, but because God wants to start
a new people, make a radical change in the story of humanity,
and that all begins with Abraham trusting the Lord by moving
from the familiar to the unfamiliar.

In the context of calling Abraham on a mission, the
Lord promises him: "I will make of you a great nation, and I
will bless you, and make your name great, so that you will be
a blessing. I will bless those who bless you, and the one who
curses you I will curse; and in you all the families of the earth
shall be blessed" (Gn 12:2-3, NRSV). While Abraham is only
one man, the Lord entrusts to him and his descendants an
awesome responsibility: They will be the carriers of blessing
for the whole of humanity. Through Abraham, *everyone* can
be blessed. Yet notice that in the midst of such a hope-filled
promise, God the Judge shows up, promising curses on whoever curses Abraham. Often, we're tempted to dismiss these
passages as merely representing the "God of the Old Testa-

ment." We don't like to think of God cursing anyone, but here the reason for this negative side to the promises is clear: Abraham is the vessel of universal blessing for all of humanity, by cursing or harming him, one is in effect, cursing and harming *all* of humanity. Abraham deserves some divine backup!

Choosing One for the Many

Now it might seem odd to make one man and his children the instrument through which all of humanity will be blessed by God, but St. Paul explains to us that in his wisdom God chose this particular people through his "purpose of election" (Rom 9:11). The idea is that Abraham and his descendants, the Israelites and the Jews, and their story reveal to all of humanity what God is like. God showed himself to them in special ways throughout their history so that he might be shown to all of humanity. They set an example, show the way, and receive the "oracles of God" (Rom 3:2) so they might be handed on to all of humankind. God's purpose of election is not restrictive and confining, trying to keep salvation a secret for the few. Rather, his purpose is open, fruitful, and universal. By choosing a particular people and walking with them, he brings salvation to all. We'll look at the theology of election more deeply later, but it is important to see here that God the Savior saves his people over and over again throughout the story of the Bible, what some refer to as "salvation history."

One of those significant moments of salvation comes after the Israelites have been enslaved by Egypt for hundreds of years. Rather than forgetting about his promises to Abraham, Isaac, and Jacob and letting his people live in perpetual servitude, the Lord interrupts. He powerfully reveals himself to Moses at the burning bush and brings harsh judgments on the Egyptians for holding the Israelites in bondage. Notice how judgment and salvation often go hand in hand. In this case, God the Savior is rescuing the Israelites from Egypt while simultaneously acting as God the Judge, who punishes evildoers.

Yikes! "Punishing evildoers" sounds judgmental, harsh, even unfair. That's a gut reaction that leaps up in most of us when we think of God the Judge, but we have to admit that God the Judge is one and the same with God the Savior. We can't separate the two. In fact, it is precisely *by his judgment* that God brings salvation. God's kind of saving is not about smoothing over the facts so that everybody has a compromised, wobbly stance. Rather, saving comes at a cost, and that cost includes judgment and punishment. Only by righting the wrong, undoing the evil or oppressive situation, and holding those responsible to account is real salvation attained. If God tried to "save" the Israelites without judging the Egyptians and taking away their slaves, then he would not have saved anyone at all. Salvation can be arrived at only through a process of judgment.

God's kind of saving is not about smoothing over the facts so that everybody has a compromised, wobbly stance. Rather, saving comes at a cost, and that cost includes judgment and punishment.

Many times in the Bible, God reaches down to save a person or a people, but usually with a judgment against an oppressor. For example, God saves the young men out of the fiery furnace to the great embarrassment of Nebuchadnezzar. God saves David, but allows Saul to be killed. God saves Elijah, but destroys one hundred men who are trying to kill him (2 Kgs 1:9-12). God helps his people begin conquering the Promised Land, but at the expense of the Canaanites. God saves the Persian Jews while their persecutor, Haman, is executed (Est 7:10). However, sometimes God judges his own people for their sins and punishes them through plague, famine, or even war. What all these instances and more show us is that God is not limited to being a judge *or* a savior. In fact, his power, his goodness, his wisdom all come together as he demonstrates his justice by saving those unjustly oppressed and as he demonstrates his saving power by judging justly.

PART II

The Devil in the Details

PART II

The Devil in the Details

Chapter 6

Does God Kill People?

Death bothers us. Why shouldn't it? All of us are headed there eventually. Unlike our ancestors, we like to keep death out of sight. When a relative dies, his or her body is quickly swept off to the funeral home for embalming, viewing, and burial. Our ancestors had home funerals, rather than funeral homes. They would invite their friends and relatives to pay their last respects in the living room of the deceased, rather than at an arm's-length facility. Saints, especially mystics, are often pictured with a skull nearby, and, supposedly, a holy man would keep a cranium on his desk as a constant reminder of our inescapable destiny. Recently, I visited a church in Rome with an impressively creepy example of this habit. The church is called *Santa Maria della Concezione dei Cappuccini*. Underneath the main church, in the crypt, are the skeletons of four thousand Capuchin friars, which have been artistically arranged in designs and patterns of femurs, pelvises, and skulls. While such comfortableness with death is disturbing to us, I have to admit that the display had its intended effect on me: There's nothing better than a stack of skulls to remind you of your fate!

The Contradiction of Death

Death bothers us because we don't understand it. It seems to contradict everything we know and feel to be right deep inside. It is disturbing because it undoes what is done. It is the opposite of life, and we have a hard time handling opposites in our minds. We'll refer to a dying person as becoming "reconciled with death" or an older person as "coming to grips" with death. When we think of death, there's something that leaps up inside of us and cries out, "It's not fair!" Some of the most painful and difficult moments in life are about death: when your parent, spouse, or child dies. Death separates us from one another and seemingly brings an end to the story of our lives.

The Bible presents us with many startling examples of death. Each particular story has its significant details that demand examination, but in this chapter we will focus on the big-picture question: Does God kill people? Our questions about many events in the Bible boil down to this question, and it deserves our attention in itself. We'll survey some examples, take a look at God's role in death, and evaluate the significance of death in his saving plan. For this chapter, we will exclude times when God uses human agents to execute others and will focus solely on those examples in the Bible when God executes people himself, often using nonhuman agents.

> *When we think of death, there's something that leaps up inside of us and cries out, "It's not fair!"*

A number of times, God uses death as a punishment. Several big examples stand out, where God wipes out or "smites" large groups of people: Noah's flood, Sodom and Gomorrah, the Egyptian firstborn, the rebellion of Korah, various plagues, and the list could go on.[29] On the individual level, quite a few biblical characters are killed by God: Lot's wife, Er; Onan; Nadab and Abihu; an anonymous prophet; Ananias and Sapphira; and Herod Agrippa.[30] While, as I said, it is important for scholars to parse the individual details of each of these accounts, what is it that unites them? Well, we can see in each one of these cases a person or people reject God and thus incur his punishment. Herod allows himself to be proclaimed a god. Ananias and Sapphira try to buy their way into spiritual authority. Nadab and Abihu corrupt the worship of God, as do

Korah and his companions. The citizens of Sodom and Gomorrah also act unjustly in God's sight. Choosing against God, choosing to reject God prompts him to reject us.

Before we try to directly confront our question, let's pause for a moment and focus on death itself. Death is a big deal to us, but if you think about it, we just like to delay the inevitable. For we all know that no amount of wrinkle cream, carrot juice, or multivitamins will actually prevent the ultimate conclusion of the aging process: death. If God sometimes punishes people in the Bible with death, he is only hastening the unavoidable endpoint of life. There is no escape from death, so it is not as if he changes that reality, but only the timing. Second, in the ancient world death was everywhere. Life expectancy was very low. Infant mortality was high. The death penalty was common for all sorts of crimes. Men died in battle. Famines and plagues were frequent and lethal. Death was a much more normal part of life for the ancients. Just imagine if most of the people you knew died in their forties or fifties and only a few lucky ones made it much past that. In a world where death was so commonplace, the fact that God would employ it as a punishment is a bit less shocking. Last, it is easy for us to think that death is the end of the story, but it is not. Death is the separation of the soul from the body. The Bible is very clear, especially in the New Testament, that life presses on after death, albeit in a changed way. Death is a moment of transformation, of leaving behind one world to come into another. It is not so much a conclusion of our life as the end of one of its chapters.

God, in his righteousness, uses death as a punishment to restore the order of justice. When people reject him, they violate his number one command: "You shall have no other gods before me." Whether that rejection takes the form of actually turning to worship an idol, as the Israelites did with the golden calf at Mount Sinai, or whether it involves thinking yourself to be more important than God, as Herod did, every act that places something above God is an idolatrous one. In fact, the primary metaphor the Bible uses to describe idolatry is *adultery*. God describes himself as married to his people, so when they reject him and pursue another god, they "commit adultery" with that god.[31] Imagine if your spouse came into your office and found a picture of your secretary on your desk instead of him or her. It would be impossible to explain away. The harm to your marriage would be done. When we reject the true God by embracing a false one, it's the same idea: rejecting our true Spouse for something or someone else. When we reject the Author of Life, death is the only answer. In the Bible stories, God allows people the freedom to reject him with their choices against life and then delivers what they desire: death.

In love God created us and the world we live in. To reject him is to reject ourselves, our Maker, our environment, and being itself.

Judging God

At times, we're even tempted to judge God against some standard of morality that pretends he is just like one of us, but he's not. When we have a gut reaction against God killing people in the Bible, often we're thinking of him as if he were a human king selfishly demanding worship like a megalomaniac. In this case, we're trying to put a moral law above God, rather than realizing that he is the source of the moral law. When we seek to hold God to a moral standard, we implicitly acknowledge the existence of the moral law, but how could there be a moral law without a moral Lawgiver? This is the crux of the problem.

God is that Lawgiver, and his acts are in accord with the moral law. He is sovereign over life and death, and each one of us draws our next breath only because God allows it. He not only created us but holds us in existence from one moment to the next. As St. Paul said, "In him we live and move and have our being" (Acts 17:28). Our very existence depends upon his will. He alone is eternal and necessary. He created us freely out of love, not obligation, so our "right to life" is contingent, limited by the sovereign will of God.

What all this means is that the acts of God we see in the Bible can and must be squared with the moral law. God's ways might be mysterious, but they are not nonsensical. In fact, in each case of God killing people, we can point to his justice. God the Judge inflicts death as a punishment for rejecting him. In that way he confirms the will of those who have chosen against him by giving them what they want: a world without God. Since God the Judge is perfectly just, the punishment always fits the crime. Serious sin against God demands serious punishment since rejecting him means rejecting the nature of the moral universe we inhabit. Rejecting God is not like rejecting another human person, but like protesting against the very fabric of our nature. In love God created us and the world we live in. To reject him is to reject ourselves, our Maker, our environment, and being itself. Proclaiming anything else as God—whether Baal, money, sex, power, or oneself—amounts to ultimately turning away from him who created us out of love and desires to draw us back to himself. It is to place the creature above the Creator, to devote the nobility of human existence to futile pursuits, to reject the dignity of worshiping God for the disgrace of wallowing in the muck of our own selfishness.

The Origin of Death

The Bible shows us time and again that "the wages of sin is death" (Rom 6:23). When we reject God, he allows us to turn away from him by handing us our just deserts. Sadly, all of us will die because of sin. Death, even in the case of those who will be redeemed, is a punishment for sin. Originally, Adam and Eve were not subject to death, but now that humanity is fallen all of us are subject to death. Because of sin, "death reigned," and all of us were under its thumb. When God rains down death on the wicked in the Bible, it is within the plan of his divine justice. Death was the due punishment for sin. As we tend to acknowledge at funerals or during crises, God has power over life and death. He has the power to give life and to take it away. Job said during his time of suffering, "The LORD gave, and the LORD has taken away; blessed be the name of the LORD" (Jb 1:21). The point is not that God's power trumps what is right, but that the exhibition of his power in the Bible is always consistent with his goodness and justice. He never commits evil acts, but when he inflicts death as a punishment, he always acts in accord with his goodness.

An example from the Gospels illustrates the nature of death as a just punishment for sin. When people question Jesus about a couple of particular terrible fates, his response is surprising:

> There were some present at that very time who told him of the Galileans whose blood Pilate had mingled with their sacrifices. And he answered them, "Do you think that these Galileans were worse sinners than all the other Galileans, because they suffered thus? I tell you, No; but unless you repent you will all likewise perish. Or those eighteen upon whom the tower in Siloam fell and killed them, do you think that they were worse offenders than all the others who dwelt in Jerusalem? I tell you, No; but unless you repent you will all likewise perish." (Lk 13:1-5)

Notice that Jesus does not say that the people whose blood was desecrated or those on whom a tower fell were poor innocent victims. Instead, he points his finger at the crowd and says, "You must repent or you will perish too!" He does not reinterpret the fates of those who died as nonmoral or having nothing to do with their sins. Rather, death for him is the logical, necessary, and just consequence of sin. Only by repenting of our sin, by turning away from it, can we avoid that consequence.

So the answer is yes, sometimes God does kill people, but he does so in accord with justice, with goodness, even with his saving love. Indeed, he "did not spare his own Son but gave him up for us all" (Rom 8:32). Mercifully, God the Judge acts as God the Savior by handing down a death sentence not to us sinners, but to his very own innocent Son.

Chapter 7

Does God Want People to Kill People?

No!

This is an important point to make: God does *not* want people to kill people. In fact, this rule is enshrined in the Ten Commandments: "Thou shalt not kill." God is the Creator, the Author of Life, and to kill a person is to undo what he has done, to reject his authorship. Taking a life robs not only the victim, but robs all of creation of that individual's personal contribution and love. Killing opposes human dignity, stealing away life from the one who lives, from his or her family, from God himself. Destroying what God has created and called good is the opposite of what he wants for us and how he created the universe to be.

Murder and the Death Penalty

So then you might be wondering why we have to ask the question at all. The problem is that occasionally in the Bible God commands killing. If killing is opposed to the life God created, then why does he sometimes mandate the death penalty in the Old Testament? On top of it, how can we square his command *not* to kill in general with his command *to kill* in specific situations? In this chapter, we'll take a look at a few examples of God using human agents to execute people, saving the Canaanite problem for the next chapter. Again, this will only be an introduction to the problem as we find it in the Old Testament. Volumes of moral theology, ethics, and just-war theory have been written on all the intricacies of these questions. Our goal is to try to make sense of the biblical narrative in an introductory way.

Some specific examples will help set the stage for our discussion. The primordial mention of the death penalty shows up in Genesis 4. Cain has just murdered his brother, Abel, and God is punishing him with banishment. Cain fears that someone will murder him probably in blood vengeance, but the Lord responds: "'Not so! If any one slays Cain, vengeance shall be taken on him sevenfold.' And the LORD put a mark on Cain, lest any who came upon him should kill him" (Gn 4:15). While the sevenfold vengeance God promises does not explicitly mention the death penalty, one can be sure that there are few fates seven times worse than death that don't include death! So what do we make of it? God institutes the death penalty in this case in order to put Cain's mind at ease since Cain fears retributive vengeance.

Vengeance comes up multiple times in the Old Testament. Understanding what ancient Near Eastern blood vengeance looked like will help frame our discussion of the death penalty. When someone committed a crime in the ancient world—say someone murdered one of your family members—you couldn't just call 911 and watch the flashing lights show up in your driveway. In fact, you might not even be able to run to the local authorities—they didn't necessarily have personnel or resources to deal with serious crime. There were no effective police forces, no prison systems, no walnut-paneled courtrooms, so getting justice for you and yours might look a bit more Old West-style than our present-day version of justice. You would probably have to organize a band of armed men, perhaps with the blessing of the local elders, to search out the criminal and bring him to justice. In the Old West, ranchers would similarly form vigilante posses to find and hang cattle rustlers who were stealing their livelihood, their cows. Ancient Near Easterners would have had to rely on their relatives and community members to see that justice was served.

Apostasy

Other examples of divinely mandated Old Testament killing are more direct than Cain's story. After the Israelites apostatize by worshiping the golden calf, Moses gathers a posse of Levites and charges them, "Thus says the LORD God of Israel, 'Put every man his sword on his side, and go to and fro from gate to gate throughout the camp, and slay every man his brother, and every man his companion, and every man his neighbor'" (Ex 32:27). Later, after another instance of pagan worship, Moses charges the leaders of the Israelites, "Every one of you slay his men who have yoked themselves to Baal of Peor" (Nm 25:5). Last, the prophet Elijah, after his famous contest with the prophets of Baal on Mount Carmel, personally executes the prophets of the false god: "And Elijah said to them, 'Seize the prophets of Baal; let not one of them escape.' And they seized them; and Elijah brought them down to the brook Kishon, and killed them there" (1 Kgs 18:40). The text tells us earlier that there were four hundred fifty prophets of Baal (18:22).

> *There are too many instances of divinely mandated killing for us to ignore. They must be explained, not explained away.*

While we can't pretend that these events don't trouble us, we must seek an explanation rather than shrug. Our temptation will be to say that they are unhistorical, that Moses and Elijah were confused, that God didn't really want these things to happen. But the trouble with that view is that it places us above God, judging his actions in salvation history in accord with our inner sense of justice, rather than allowing him to teach us through his actions. Besides, what we see in these instances is consistent with the justice theology of the

Old Testament in general, which we encountered in the last chapter. Even if the historicity of these and other accounts can be challenged or attenuated based on literary or archaeological grounds, the fact is that there are too many instances of divinely mandated killing for us to ignore. They must be explained, not explained away.

That said, the instances I cited are all connected with pagan worship: the golden calf, Baal of Peor, and Baal. In each of these three instances, the people of God are caught up in worship of false deities. The Lord mandates the death penalty for those involved and uses an official, yet relatively informal, way of executing his will using a posse of Levites, the organization of tribal elders, and even a lone prophet. God's use of human agents does not endorse wanton killing, but rather limits the spread of killing by isolating it within the system of divine justice. The only permitted killing in the Old Testament that is not prohibited by the Ten Commandments is that which God explicitly mandates. To execute justice with God's authority is not murder, but to take the law into one's own hands and kill without his mandate is. The Lord's death sentence came upon those who had rejected the real God, the Creator, and had joined their fates to false gods, which St. Paul tells us are not actually gods but demons (1 Cor 10:2). Idolatry, as we saw in the last chapter, is adultery against the true God, against the one who made us. By worshiping idols, people defy the Author of Life and choose death. Again, "the wages of sin is death" (Rom 6:23). By mandating the death penalty, the Lord grants idolaters that which they ask for: to be separated from him.

What Is the Lesson of the Death Penalty?

Now the death penalty is an imperfect form of justice. (Notice that Jesus drives out the money-changers from the Temple, but does not execute them.) However, the death penalty is essential to the divine pedagogy, the gradual revelation of God to man. The death penalty in the Old Testament reveals to us the deadly gravity of sin. St. Paul explains this aspect of the divine pedagogy when talking about the Law of Moses: "It was sin, working death in me through what is good [the law], in order that sin might be shown to be sin, and through the commandment might become sinful beyond measure" (Rom 7:13). The holy law of the Old Testament reveals the utter sinfulness of sin, the existential horror of choosing against our very own Creator, the fact that sin makes us enemies of God and friends with death.

In fact, the Old Testament death penalty is a visible sign of the invisible reality to be revealed—that mortal sin is worse than physical death.

The death-oriented nature of sin is the ultimate lesson of the death penalty in the Old Testament. In fact, the Old Testament death penalty is a visible sign of the invisible reality to be revealed—that mortal sin is worse than physical death. As Jesus says: "And do not fear those who kill the body but cannot kill the soul. Rather fear him who can destroy both soul and body in hell" (Mt 10:28). He's telling his disciples not to fear mere human persecutors, but to *fear God*. God is the one who can "destroy both soul and body." His judgment is far more fearful than the tortures of human bullies. Physical death is a trifle compared with everlasting punishment.

While the Ten Commandments ban killing, it is important to note a few legitimate exceptions to the rule for our own era. First, it is possible that in order to defend oneself as a private citizen, or to defend society as a public official, one may need to strike a fatal blow.[32] For example, in 1984 a mass shooter killed twenty people and wounded twenty others at a San Diego McDonald's before being shot and killed by a SWAT team sniper. Second, the Church does allow the death penalty as a legitimate punishment of a criminal offender if no other means can be found to prevent the person from continuing to gravely harm society.[33] However, as I mentioned in the last chapter, the popes have recently expressed skepticism that the death penalty is still necessary in modern societies where life imprisonment effectively contains offenders. Last, sometimes circumstances legitimately call for military defense. The *Catechism* outlines some of the "just war" doctrine's specific requirements, which limit the scope of warfare to responding to aggression as a last resort with real prospects for success without producing worse evils than those inflicted by the aggressor.[34]

In sum, God loudly and clearly forbids killing. However, there are a few circumstances in the Old Testament where he employs human agents to carry out the death penalty, usually in connection with sins of idolatry. Idolatry is a grave evil that promotes false gods above the true Author of Life. By punishing idolaters with the death penalty, God reveals to us the utter sinfulness of sin—that choosing false gods is choosing death and separation from the source of our life. Finally, in very limited circumstances, killing another person may be legitimately justified in order to defend society. These reflections will prepare us to discuss a dramatic example of human agents killing others in God's name: the conquest of the Canaanites.

Chapter 8

Killing the Canaanites: Genocide or Judgment?

One of the most troubling pictures in our imagining of biblical times is that of a raiding party of Israelite soldiers attacking a Canaanite village as if they were Vikings, pillaging and killing indiscriminately. Men, women, animals, even children, fall as they mercilessly slaughter one after another. Two horrific questions rise in us at once: How could anyone kill in the name of God? How on earth could God actually *want* his people to do such things?

In this chapter, we will respond to these questions by offering a few different observations. First, we will examine the literary and historical evidence to see what God actually commanded and how it was or was not carried out. Second, we will revisit this imaginative picture to see if it gets the biblical portrait right. Along the way, we'll find quite a few facts that will modify that picture. Lastly, we will dwell on the tough theological questions that arise from the Israelites' killing of the Canaanites, saving the specific and important question of killing children for the next chapter.

The Command to Conquer

God's original command to conquer Canaan with *herem*[35] warfare comes in a section of Deuteronomy dealing with laws of warfare:

But in the cities of these peoples that the LORD your God gives you for an inheritance, you shall save alive nothing that breathes, but you shall utterly destroy them, the Hittites and the Amorites, the Canaanites and the Perizzites, the Hivites and the Jebusites, as the LORD your God has commanded; that they may not teach you to do according to all their abominable practices which they have done in the service of their gods, and so to sin against the LORD your God. (Dt 20:16-18)

This original command is clear enough: kill everyone and everything in the cities of the Promised Land. It is important to note that the justification for this "ban" is that the peoples who inhabit the land might teach the Israelites to follow their false religion and worship false gods. Earlier in Deuteronomy, the death penalty is prescribed for false prophets, relatives, friends, and whole cities who incite others to worship false gods (Chapter 13). However, the ban command appears as something of a Plan B. The original plan included God himself in cooperation with the Israelites driving out the Canaanites from the land gradually so that the fields would not lie fallow (Ex 23:27-33). The war itself seeks to secure Abraham's claim on the Promised Land. God had sworn the land to him, and the Israelites enter to enforce that oath.

The Lord brings judgment on the Canaanites' culture and religion but waits for centuries for them to turn to him before he acts. It is not an impatient move.

Note also that the Deuteronomy 20 passage limits the ban to "the cities." The Hebrew word for city, '*îr*, deserves to be explained. A city in the ancient world would not have looked like a modern metropolis with skyscrapers and suburbs. Rather, ancient cities in general were quite small walled settlements. In the Near East, they would house centers of government and religion, and often they would have an emergency food storage supply—like the centralized granaries in the Joseph story. Most people were farmers and lived in unwalled villages or hamlets near their farms. Before very recent modern times, farming was the ubiquitous occupation. For example, at the time of the founding of the United States, ninety percent of the total labor force worked on farms.[36] The vast majority of the population in ancient Canaan did not live in cities, but in the countryside. The city functioned more like a fort—a stronghold where a defense force could make a stand against an invading army.[37]

But why would God command such a conquest, even if it was limited to fortlike cities? Interestingly, the *herem* warfare command in Deuteronomy 20 has much earlier origins in the Genesis story of Abraham. In the midst of promising the land of Canaan to Abraham, God informs him that this real estate deal will have to be postponed for four hundred years to give the Canaanites time to repent, "for the iniquity of the Amorites [a Canaanite people group] is not yet complete" (Gn 15:16). The Lord brings judgment on the Canaanites' culture and religion but waits for centuries for them to turn to him before he acts. It is not an impatient move.

The Canaanites

We have already encountered God the Judge and seen how he sometimes uses lethal force to enact justice, so what did the Canaanites do to deserve his wrath? The other deadly divine judgments we have looked at were responses to acts of false worship, where people chose to devote themselves to a false god instead of the true one. In the Canaanites' case, they worshiped a group of gods by means of some strange practices, which originate in stories about those gods. Leviticus 18 mentions some of these practices explicitly and warns the Israelites not to engage in them: incest, bestiality, adultery, child sacrifice. In addition, the Old Testament evidence shows that the Canaanite religion also included both male and female cult prostitution.[38] The Lord brings judgment down against this Canaanite culture of false worship and abhorrent sexual practices. Notably, the main goal of the ban is to destroy the Canaanite religion and its attendant beliefs and practices so that the Israelites themselves will not fall into false worship. The Lord knows the weaknesses of his people and realizes that a harsh elimination of temptation to false worship is the best way to eradicate the duplicity in their hearts. The Old Testament book of Wisdom reflects on God's decision to judge the Canaanites and their religion:

> Those who dwelt of old in thy holy land thou didst hate for their detestable practices, their works of sorcery and unholy rites, their merciless slaughter of children, and their sacrificial feasting on human flesh and blood. These initiates from the midst of a heathen cult, these parents who murder helpless lives, thou didst will to destroy by the hands of our fathers, that the land most precious of all to thee might receive a worthy colony of the servants of God. (Wis 12:3-7)

From Wisdom's perspective, God's decision was rooted in a response to the ritualization of sexual abuse and child-killing. While Wisdom might overplay the horror of the Canaanites' practices (other evidence does not confirm the cannibalism mentioned here), the ban's intention is clear: to eliminate an evil religion and the culture that produced it. Wisdom also points out the long-suffering patience of God, who waited for the Canaanites to repent and at first punished them "little by little" to try to change their hearts:

> But even these thou didst spare, since they were but men, and didst send wasps as forerunners of thy army, to destroy them little by little, though thou wast not un-

able to give the ungodly into the hands of the righteous in battle, or to destroy them at one blow by dread wild beasts or thy stern word. But judging them little by little *thou gavest them a chance to repent*, though thou wast not unaware that their origin was evil and their wickedness inborn, and that their way of thinking would never change. (Wis 12:8-10, emphasis added)

Before implementing a last-resort plan of judgment, God granted the Canaanites ample time to repent and turn away from their evil practices. But because they persisted, the Lord decided to punish their culture and destroy their religion using human agents.

The Israelites: God's Agents

The Israelites, the Lord's human agents, do act on his command but never fully implement the ban. The texts continually emphasize the incompleteness of the conquest and how the Canaanites persist in the land after the conquest period. Jericho is the earliest example we have of Israel actually trying to implement the ban. In that instance we are told, "Then they utterly destroyed all in the city, both men and women, young and old, oxen, sheep, and asses, with the edge of the sword" (Jos 6:21). Jericho itself has been discovered by archaeologists at Tell es-Sultan. It is not a centrally located city, but a fortlike outpost on the edge of the Canaanite settlements just a few acres in size. The post-battle notice in Joshua 6:21 sounds as if it reports a genocide, but other examples of these reports in the Bible show that this one conveys information in a stereotype. The phrase *me'ish ve'ad-'ishah* ("from man to woman") is a stereotypical expression that simply means "everyone," whether both men and women were present or not.[39] If Jericho was more like a fort, housing mainly soldiers entrusted with the defense of Canaan, then the vast majority of the victims mentioned in Joshua 6:21 would be combatants. Of course, if you know your Bible well, you'll think of Rahab, the Jericho-residing prostitute who harbored the Israelite spies and who was spared from the ban. I don't need to convince you that it would not be surprising to find a prostitute near a group of soldiers, but what is surprising is that she is an exception to the rule of destruction. The "all" in Joshua 6:21 does not include Rahab or her family, which the text tells us includes "her father and mother and brothers and all who belonged to her" (Jos 6:23). While the command God gives is all-encompassing, we find in actual practice certain people are excepted from the ban.

> *The very reason God indicated for the original* herem *command—that without such a conquest his people might worship idols—is exactly what happens.*

Another example of *herem* in action is the Israelites' conquest of Ai. Archaeologists have usually identified Ai with a site called et-Tell. Trying to square the archaeological evidence with the biblical text can be very difficult. In this case, Ai was destroyed several times before Israel's conquest of Canaan. At the time of Joshua, it would have been ancient ruins, which matches its name: Ai in Hebrew means "heap of ruins." Since it is very close to the much larger city Bethel, it could be considered "a fortified outpost to protect Bethel."[40] The victory notice in the text deserves explanation: "And all who fell that day, both men and women, were twelve thousand, all the people of Ai" (Jos 8:25). Here again, we find the stock phrase "from man to woman," which indicates simply that *everyone* in the place was killed whether or not there were actually both men and women there. But twelve thousand sounds like a lot of people! As many others have explained, the word for "thousand" in Hebrew (*'elep*) is the same as the word for "a clan or a military unit."[41] In the case of the Israelites' conquest of Ai, we're more likely looking at the defeat of twelve squads of soldiers of indeterminate size, not a basketball arena full of people. This evaluation of the situation matches the archaeological evidence and fits linguistically with the biblical text.

Did the Conquest Succeed?

The Book of Joshua presents an optimistic portrait of Israel's success under Joshua's leadership. He conquered "the whole land," "all their kings" (Jos 10:40). The book insists on his comprehensive success (11:16-23). But these snapshots are belied by other information both in Joshua and Judges: "There remains very much land to possess" (Jos 13:1). The Israelites failed to drive out many of the indigenous tribes (Jos 13:13; 15:63; 16:10; 17:13). Later, in Judges, which is literarily connected with Joshua, the emphasis is on Israel's failure (Jgs 1:21, 27-36). Judges enumerates all the peoples whom Israel failed to drive out. We find that the Canaanites are still very much around, annoying the Israelites like thorns (Jgs 2:3). The very reason God indicated for the original *herem* command—that without such a conquest his people might worship idols—is exactly what happens. The Canaanites in the land persist as a constant source of temptation to false worship. The Israelites' failure to complete the conquest leads them over and over again into idolatrous worship. Notably, after Israel's failure to complete the conquest in the allotted time, God does not ask them to keep trying to drive out the Canaanites. They are to limit themselves to destroying Canaanite religion ("break down their altars," Jgs 2:2), but God will no longer "drive them out before you" (Jgs 2:3). Instead, the Canaanites stay in the land as a punishment and a relentless test of faith. Their very existence is a moral rebuke, a reminder of one's inadequacy and need for the Lord.

The divinely mandated *herem* command was time-limited for a particular moment in salvation history. It was not a general principle or law to be applied in many cases. So we, as Christians, have no right to take the law into our own hands or wage a *herem*-style war. In the last chapter, I outlined the very limited spheres in which killing people is permitted in Catholic teaching: self-defense, societal defense, and defensive war. Notice that all permitted killing is defensive in nature, while the ancient war against Canaan seems *offensive*. (It could be argued that the conquest of Canaan was *defensive* since it sought to "defend" God's promise to Abraham.) In one recent example, Catholics in Sudan have taken up arms, organizing civilian militias to defend their communities from the so-called Lord's Resistance Army.[42]

So how does all this evidence modify our imaginative picture of what Israel's conquest of Canaan really looked like? Instead of hordes of Viking pillagers burning villages, we might imagine squads of soldiers sacking fort after fort in the Canaanite hinterlands, overcoming defensive forces and destroying these fort "cities." While the hyperbolic language of some of the victory reports makes it sound as if all the inhabitants of the whole land were driven headlong into the Mediterranean before the Israelite conquerors, the not-so-optimistic texts reveal a more nuanced, incomplete conquest. The ancients' hyperbole might sound like our conversations after football games, where you might hear, "We slaughtered them!" when only touchdowns were scored.

Finally, we must pause to reflect on the theological implications of the conquest of Canaan. We have seen that God brought judgment down on the Canaanites because of their evil practices connected with the worship of false gods. Also, God appoints the Israelites as his agents of judgment rather than directly and supernaturally dealing with them. This choice is a little mysterious, but it seems to be part of the divine pedagogy in that God is training his people to eradicate all idolatry from their hearts by employing them in the active destruction of an idolatrous culture. Some early Christian interpreters who saw a spiritual lesson for us in the conquest of Canaan expanded on this particular dimension of the conquest. For them, the Canaanites represent sin and sinful inclinations in our hearts that must be totally eradicated so that God's presence can fully reign in us.

While some of the evidence can help us see the limited scope of the conquest, the ultimate question comes down to God's authority. Does he have the right to take human life and to appoint human beings to act in his name? Yes. Now, as we have already seen, all death is a punishment for sin, even the death of holy people. All human beings are subject to death. It is our enemy, our mortal foe. But our sin, our rejection of God, brings death on all of us. When God appoints the Israelites to conquer Canaan, our hearts jump. We all expect death but like to push it aside from our minds in favor of rosier things. The conquest of Canaan confronts us with our own mortality and causes us to realize the awesome, all-encompassing authority of God. Like that of Adam, to whom God said, "you are dust, and to dust you shall return" (Gn 3:19), our "right to life" is always subject to his goodness, his justice, and his timing.

Chapter 9

Killing Children?

Of all the topics we need to cover in this book on dark things in Scripture, this is the darkest. It reminds me of going into the subbasement or crawl space of a beautiful, historic building. The outside and the public spaces might be wonderfully decorated and proportional, but when one winds his way into the hidden parts of the building—the boiler room, the janitor's closet, the tunnels with pipes and wiring—one finds not frescoes but cobwebs, not buffed floors but cockroaches, dirt, and dank smells. The horror of killing innocent children cannot be overestimated. The most gut-wrenching news stories are those when children die, especially when killed by their parents or caregivers who are responsible for loving and protecting them. Killing children seems so contrary to the nature of a loving and merciful God that it feels unexplainable. Yet we cannot abandon our purpose here but must seek an answer without great hope of finding a very satisfying one.

The Old Testament contains several examples of children being killed by divine intent. While certain events imply the death of a large number of children as part of God's design—for example, the Flood, the death of the Egyptian firstborn—these stories do not explicitly mention the ages of the persons killed. However, a few examples attribute the killing of children directly to God: the death of King David's baby and the "households" (presumably including children) of Korah and his followers being swallowed by the earth (Nm 16:32). One text shows the Israelites stoning and burning Achan and his "sons and daughters" to punish him for not obeying the ban (Jos 7:24), and apparently they thus appease the wrath of God (7:1,26). Other texts indicate God appointing human agents through a prophet to kill children in his name. Exterminating everything "that breathes" (Dt 20:16) includes children, and the Israelites are reported to actually have done this (Jos 11:11,14). The prophet Samuel issues the most concrete example when he commands King Saul:

> And Samuel said to Saul, "The Lord sent me to anoint you king over his people Israel; now therefore hearken to the words of the Lord. Thus says the Lord of hosts, 'I will punish what Amalek did to Israel in opposing them on the way, when they came up out of Egypt. Now go and smite Amalek, and utterly destroy all that they have; do not spare them, but kill both man and woman, *infant and suckling*, ox and sheep, camel and ass.'" (1 Sm 15:1-3, emphasis added)

The Old Testament contains several examples of children being killed by divine intent.

This text notably includes specific vocabulary to indicate little children: infant and suckling. The last example is more of a fantasy text that envisions a future in which poetic justice is served. It comes in the course of Psalm 137, wherein the exiled psalmist is bemoaning the fate of Israel, held captive in Babylon. This lament reaches fever pitch in the concluding verses:

> Remember, O LORD, against the Edomites the day of Jerusalem,
> how they said, "Raze it, raze it! Down to its foundations!"
> O daughter of Babylon, you devastator!
> Happy shall he be who requites you with what you have done to us!

Happy shall he be who takes your little ones
and dashes them against the rock! (Ps 137:7-9)

The psalmist switches from talking to the Lord to talking to the mythical *bat-babel,* "daughter Babylon."[43] He pronounces happiness or blessing on those who gruesomely slaughter her fictive "little ones."

Sin and Death

Before we respond to these texts, it is worth saying that no matter how well we think through the problem, we are not likely to walk away from the conversation fully satisfied. Our hearts are tied up in our children, in the hope of the human race, in the beauty and innocence we so clearly see in little ones. Clear thinking can't easily trump deep feeling. However, we have to be careful not to import our cultural values that so esteem and glorify childhood and judgingly stand in self-righteous indignation against our ancient forebears. Our era has not been kind to children any more than theirs. Whether the suffering brought to children by the World Wars, the Holocaust, the terrifying AIDS epidemic in Africa which has stolen away so many parents, or even down to the extermination of the unborn at the hands of abortion practitioners, we have been unable to protect children from many evils in our time.

Sin's interpersonal effects reveal how evil it is. It can snowball into a revolting mess and affect many people, including kids.

In order to begin an explanation, we must return to one of the ideas we encountered earlier: all death is a punishment for sin. All human beings are subject to death because of our broken nature and our sinful heritage. No one can escape. In a very real sense, each of us has inherited "guilt," the conse-

quences of our first parents' sin. Children, even the tiniest unborn babies, share in this inheritance of sin. All of us will die
at some point, and that death happens only because of sin.
This means that, theologically speaking, there are no innocent
people. Everyone is subject to the "reign of death" (Rom 5:14,
17), including children. This universal theological reality of
original sin also helps explain the generational consequences
of sin. Right in the middle of the first of the Ten Commandments, God says, "For I the LORD your God am a jealous God,
visiting the iniquity of the fathers upon the children to the
third and the fourth generation of those who hate me, but
showing steadfast love to thousands of those who love me and
keep my commandments" (Ex 20:5-6). Loving God has wonderfully positive consequences of intergenerational blessing,
but rejecting God, "hating" him, has intergenerational consequences too, baleful ones. The inheritable consequences of sin
do not mean that the children inherit culpability for sin, but
only some of its nasty results. Old Testament law reflects this
by forbidding the putting of children to death for their parents' crimes (Dt 24:16; Ez 18:20). We can easily see that the
natural results of sin can be bad for kids—if a parent has an
addiction to drugs or alcohol, the child can suffer from it. If a
parent gambles away the family's money, a child will be hurt.
Sin's interpersonal effects reveal how evil it is. It can snowball
into a revolting mess and affect many people, including kids. It
shows how interconnected we are. Fortunately, this intercon-
nection has its upside: blessings too can spread from person to
person, from parent to child.

Another facet of the problem to note is that though we
are focused on answering seemingly arcane questions about
ancient history, these questions touch us very closely. The answer we give must be somewhat similar to the answer we give
to a mourning parent who has lost a child and asks us, "Why?"
The most moving and sorrowful funerals I have attended are
those of children. I remember one in which the priest himself

carried the tiny casket down the aisle and placed it before the altar. There was not a dry eye in the church. When children die, we ask why God would permit it, how it could happen, and what our response should be. Death is a moment for these kinds of reflections, and perhaps our answer to the problem of Old Testament killing of children will help us think through them.

Children and the Ancients

One crucial factor that should shape our understanding of these Old Testament passages is that the ancients viewed children not as pure, blank-slate innocents but as authentic members of their families, clans, and cultures. Children were more like "mini-adults" than unadulterated creatures. The distance between a baby and a full-grown man of military age was not seen as a giant chasm marked by milestones such as youth baseball and high school graduation. Even advertisers in our culture realize this and embed credit-card advertisements in children's board games such as Life and Monopoly to influence the decisions children will make when they enter adulthood. In ancient times, children started helping their parents with farm work and the tasks of daily life as soon as they could walk and talk. By and large, ancient children were not sent to schools but were educated in the home, on the job—and the job was the daily care of the house and farm for the whole family's sustenance. Children shared in the workload, the failures, the successes, the abundance, and the famine with their parents. They were not sheltered from what we call "the real world" but were immersed in it from birth.

The role of children as mini-adults who could pose a real threat can be seen in some modern conflicts that last for generations. For example, children in the Israeli-Palestinian conflict are taught from a young age who the enemy is and how to oppose him. They are not shielded from all forms of violence but sometimes witness or experience it. The "war" in which they are engaged is not a limited "overseas contingency operation," but is an ongoing, generations-long, life-and-death struggle for the land, for the future. The children in that conflict know which side they are on from a very young age. Other modern examples show that the killing of children is not confined to the ancient world: when the Bolsheviks overthrew the czar of Russia, they killed both him and his children so that the line could not be continued. We can also see the generational nature of violent conflict in the famous Hatfield-McCoy feud, which lasted for about forty years.

Did the Israelites Actually Kill Children?

Several factors limit the actual extent of the Israelites' conquest of Canaan and therefore their role in killing children. First, as we saw before, the original commandment to conquer the land in Deuteronomy 20 presents an ideal picture that is never really fulfilled. Israel does not systematically exterminate Canaanites or even successfully drive them from the land. Instead, they attack "cities," which are essentially military targets and are only sometimes reported as actually implementing the ban. When they do, *only once* are we actually told anything about the ages of the conquered: "Then they utterly destroyed all in the city, both men and women, *young and old*, oxen, sheep, and asses, with the edge of the sword" (Jos 6:21, emphasis added). The Hebrew phrase used here is *minna'ar ve'adzaqen*, "from young to old." The word *na'ar*, young, can mean "young man, manservant." While sometimes it is used to denote young boys, it is also used to indicate those past puberty. For example, in Genesis 19:4, the same stereotypical phrase ("from young to old") is used to describe the crowd gathering around Lot's house in Sodom to gang-rape his guests. The use of the phrase in Joshua 6:21, which describes the aftermath of the battle for Jericho, simply indicates that everyone found in that fort city was killed regardless of age, but it does not necessarily mean that children actually were present.[44]

Herem *warfare, which included the killing of children, was not foreign to ancient Near Eastern cultures.*

When the Lord includes children in his judgment against the Canaanites or Amalekites, we must take into account the cultural circumstances as much as possible. *Herem* warfare, which included the killing of children, was not foreign to ancient Near Eastern cultures. For example, when the prophet Elisha anoints Hazael as king of Syria, he forecasts that Hazael will attack Israel and "you will set on fire their fortresses, and you will slay their young men with the sword, and *dash in pieces their little ones, and rip up their women with child*" (2 Kgs 8:12, emphasis added). Similarly, Isaiah prophesies about how the Medes will treat the Babylonians when they conquer them: "*Their infants will be dashed in pieces* before their eyes; their houses will be plundered and their wives ravished. Behold, I am stirring up the Medes against them, who have no regard for silver and do not delight in gold. Their bows will slaughter the young men; they will have no mercy on the fruit of the womb; *their eyes will not pity children*" (Is 13:16-18, emphasis added). Also, the prophet Nahum recounts the destruction of Assyria's capital Nineveh in this way: "Yet she was carried away, she went into captivity; *her little ones were dashed in pieces* at the head of every street; for her honored men lots were cast, and all her great men were bound in chains (Na 3:10, emphasis added).

These examples of other nations carrying out similar deeds of killing children provide an important cultural background for understanding Israel's use of *herem* warfare. The conquest of a nation would often include a means for preventing that nation from coming back—whether by killing the children, deporting people (as the Babylonians did to the Jews), or by forcing intermarriage (as the Assyrians did to the Israelites). Ancient Near Eastern cultures in general did not have the organization, will, or resources to handle child refugee crises, so they resorted to other means for dealing with child victims in a conflict. This cultural element explains at least part of God's command to attack the Amalekites in 1 Samuel 15:3.

> *This must be one of the harshest lessons of the divine pedagogy—that rejecting God can lead to the condemnation of an entire people, including kids.*

That passage cites an earlier instance in which the Amalekites, generations earlier, had sought to prevent the Israelites from entering Canaan. The first battle with the Amalekites occurs when the Lord gives the battle to Israel as long as Moses keeps his hands raised in the air (Ex 17:8-16). Later, the Amalekites rout a disobedient Israel (Nm 14:45) and even the syncretistic prophet Balaam forecasts their destruction (Nm 24:20). Toward the end of Moses' last Deuteronomy speech, he commands the Israelites to attack Amalek after they have completed the conquest of Canaan (Dt 25:17-19). Later, in the Judges period, the Amalekites again fight against Israel (Jgs 3:13; 6:3). When King Saul does war against Amalek, he does not fully implement the ban but keeps alive some of the best animals and the king of Amalek. For his duplicity in executing the Lord's command, he is stripped of the kingship (1 Sm 15:26; 28:18). And while the text makes it sound as if absolutely every Amalekite besides the king was eliminated (1 Sm 15:8), we can see that this was not the case since Amalekites show up later in the narrative (1 Sm 27:8; 30:1,13; 2 Sm 1:8). Also, the battlefield of Saul's victory ranged "from Havilah as far as Shur, which is east of Egypt" (1 Sm 15:7). This territory would extend from modern-day Kuwait almost to Egypt—an impossibly large battlefield, including territory of about six modern nation-states. These factors clue us in that the narrative in 1 Samuel 15 exaggerates some parts of the story for literary purposes. They do not eliminate the difficulty of God commanding the slaughter of "infant and suckling," but perhaps they limit how literally we should read this order.

Finding the End of the Story

These reflections might help us put the ancient Israelites' killing of children in historical perspective, but I doubt they bring us to a place of perfect peace. The killing of children is deeply troubling to us, and even the strongest logic cannot reduce the irreducibly awful. This must be one of the harshest lessons of the divine pedagogy—that rejecting God can lead to the condemnation of an entire people, including kids. We must come back to two ideas that will help us to theologically bookend the question of the Old Testament killing of children. First, God is the master of life and death. He is the Creator; we are the created. He is the Necessary, Ultimate Being, and we are contingent creatures living in the world he created. All of our lives, even our next breath, depend upon him holding us in being, keeping us alive, keeping all of reality together. Without him, there is nothing at all. So all human life is dependent on God, and he can give it and take it away without any legitimate objection on our part. We have no "right to life" apart from his will. Yet God is not a bully. All of his perfections are held together in his Being at once. He is simultaneously good and fierce, just and merciful. His character provides us with reasons for fear, for awe, and yet also for hope, for trust. In C. S. Lewis' *The Lion, the Witch and the Wardrobe*, one of the children asks Mr. Beaver about the lion, Aslan (the Christ-figure in the book), "Is he safe?" Mr. Beaver responds, "Safe?... Don't you hear what Mrs. Beaver tells you? Who said anything about safe? 'Course he isn't safe. But he's good."

Last, death is not the end of the story. Though death reigns for a time, its reign will be brought to an end. In fact, Jesus triumphed over death already and we live in the in-between time before death is fully subjected to the victory of life. For the children who died in Old Testament conflicts, whether at the hands of the Israelites, the Amalekites, the Syrians, or the Medes, we don't know their final destination, but we do know that their souls are immortal and that God is merciful. We cannot presume that they are saved, but like all children who have died without baptism, "the liturgy of the Church invites us to trust in God's mercy and to pray for their salvation."[45] The darkest moments in life call for the deepest trust in God. If our God can create the universe and bring something out of nothing, then he can take care of all those who suffer and bring about justice for all, even for little children.

Chapter 10

Child Sacrifice

Imagine a mother with tears in her eyes fiercely hugging her infant for the last time, clutching him close. Then with deliberation, she pulls the baby away from her body and hands him to the priestess who, despite his screams and cries, places him into the awaiting bronze hands of the god.[46] Next, as he arches his back to avoid the flames, the child falls from the brazen hands into the firepit itself. The mother's tears do not diminish even after the screams have died away.

Many children were sacrificed in this way in the ancient world. Thousands of child sacrificial victims have been found in ancient Carthage, on the north coast of Africa. Their bones attest to the long persistence of child sacrifice for religious reasons. While scholars debate how to interpret the archaeological evidence for child sacrifice in the ancient Near East, it is clear that many cultures around the Mediterranean practiced some form of human sacrifice and that this often included the sacrifice of children. For vignettes of child sacrifice to make it into the Bible is not surprising, but the question is not merely about history, but about God. Did God ever *want* anybody to sacrifice children to him as a form of worship?

The Binding of Isaac

The prime example is the story of the "Binding" of Isaac. After many years of following God more or less faithfully, Abraham has finally received the child of promise, the one who will carry forth his line and on whom the promises of God will dwell: Isaac. Isaac's miraculous and long-anticipated birth is attended by celebration and happiness. Finally, Abraham has an heir. Finally, the story of salvation can move forward. But in Genesis 22, "God tested Abraham." That puts it a bit mildly. In no uncertain terms, God commands Abraham, "Take your son, your only son Isaac, whom you love, and go to the land of Moriah and offer him there as a burnt offering on one of the mountains of which I shall tell to you" (v. 2). What? God is the one who called Abraham. God is the one who promised him an heir. God is the one who helped him and Sarah to conceive in their old age. He asks a lot of Abraham, but why this? It makes no sense!

At the climax of the narrative, when Abraham has the knife raised to slay Isaac, an angel interrupts and commands him to stop. Why would God command him to sacrifice Isaac in the first place if he was just going to call it all off in the end?

Abraham, however, does not hesitate. He saddles his donkey, brings his servants and his son. He makes his way to the appointed mountain and starts climbing up with Isaac. His alacrity in obeying is remarkable considering his earlier hesitations and protestations at certain points: He had objected to God's judgment of Sodom and Gomorrah (Gn 18:22-33). He also resisted his wife's request, and God had to intervene to convince him (Gn 21:11-12). So why does he capitulate now and just roll along as if everything is normal? This question and a few other details might help us sort out what's going on here.

The story doesn't say how old Isaac is, but it does say that he carried the firewood for the sacrifice up the mountain (22:6). That means we're dealing with at least a teenager. He can't be a baby if he's hoofing a pile of wood up a mountain. If he's strong enough to do that, then why doesn't he just overpower his father and run away? Thinking through these incongruities has to shape our reading of what's going on. At the climax of the narrative, when Abraham has the knife raised to slay Isaac, an angel interrupts and commands him to stop. Why would God command him to sacrifice Isaac in the first place if he was just going to call it all off in the end?

The story tells us its purpose twice: God wanted to test Abraham (22:1) and then to reaffirm the point as the angel says, "Now I know that you fear God, seeing you have not withheld your son, your only son, from me" (22:12). Thus, on the one hand, it is a test of Abraham's faith. Does he really trust in God? However, this whole child sacrifice affair seems like a rather awkward way to go about proving his fidelity. Why not send him through a financial crisis or even, like Job, submit him to severe suffering to see if he remains faithful?

I think if we look closely we can see two deeper dimensions to this story that can help us make sense of it. First, the test of faith, which is an obvious part of the narrative, may be more subtle than it appears—that is, perhaps God is revealing something to Abraham about his own heart. He wants Abraham to put his whole trust in God, to rely totally on him and not to rely on worldly things. It would be easy for Isaac to become something of an idol for Abraham: the hope of the future, the only son, the child of promise. He could start to emphasize the importance of Isaac to the exclusion of God, rather than continually receive him as a gift from God. We can do the same thing with the people, gifts, and things that God has entrusted to our care. If we start to treat these things as gods in themselves, we can lose sight of the God who gave them to us in the first place.

Second, God might be teaching an even deeper lesson here. Child sacrifice was a common practice in Abraham's time. Many religions in his milieu thought that sacrificing children was a legitimate way to relate to the divine. To win a battle, to make it rain, to promote fertility, killing children as part of a religious ritual was seen as a normal way to prompt the gods to act. The drama and horror of it made it the height of religious ritual. Weirdly, in our story, Isaac appears as a strong young man, so it seems that not only Abraham, but also Isaac himself consented to the ritual and was ready to go along with it. The text tells us that Abraham "bound" his son before putting him on the altar, so it is possible that he had to overpower him to do so, but a virile young man could probably fight off a century-old patriarch. My money would be on Isaac. Whether Isaac consented or not, Abraham certainly did. He must have been somewhat surprised when the angel interrupted, but there is evidence that he might have known what was happening all along. When he and Isaac leave the servants behind, he says, "*we* will come back to you" (v. 5, NRSV). Perhaps he knew that Isaac would come down from the mountain alive, but he was willing to go through with the mountaintop slaughter. At the crucial moment, God stops him and Abraham takes Isaac off the altar and sacrifices a nearby ram, which God provided as a substitute. The deeper lesson here is simple: God does not want to be worshiped with human sacrifices. Abraham might have known this on one level, but God wanted to impress this important principle deeply into his heart and mind so that he and his descendants would not be tempted to imitate their pagan neighbors.

Last, Abraham's near sacrifice of Isaac points to a greater moment later in the story, when another young man will climb a hill, carrying wood on his back, and die as a sacrifice by the will of his father, but that's another story.

Other Old Testament Texts on Child Sacrifice

So if the Binding of Isaac is not an endorsement of child sacrifice, but a condemnation of it, then how does that track with other Old Testament texts? Eight times, the Old Testament mentions a god named Molech, to whom child sacrifices were apparently offered. Now, there is scholarly debate about the identity of this god and whether the term was a name for a god or for the ritual of child sacrifice. But the Bible is unequivocal in rejecting all Molech offerings as abominable: "You shall not give any of your children to devote them by fire to Molech, and so profane the name of your God: I am the LORD" (Lv 18:21). In fact, biblical law demands the death penalty for any parent who sacrifices his children to Molech (Lv 20:2-5) and condemns the practice multiple times (Dt 12:31; 18:10-12). God's teaching on this matter is straightforward. However, as is often the case in the Old Testament, obedience is the issue.

The Bible generally labels child sacrifice as a practice used in the worship of foreign deities. For example, Psalm 106 says, "They sacrificed their sons / and their daughters to the demons; / they poured out innocent blood, / the blood of their sons and daughters, / whom they sacrificed to the idols of Canaan; / and the land was polluted with blood" (vv. 37-38). Here it seems simple enough: that child sacrifice was a pagan form of worship. But there are other biblical instances where the problem lies closer to home, where some Israelites are using child sacrifice as a false way to worship the true God. For example, Leviticus 20:3 mentions "defiling my sanctuary and profaning my holy name." Later, Jeremiah prophesies against those who "burn their sons and their daughters in the fire; which I did not command" (Jer 7:31). In addition, Ezekiel 20:31 seems to suggest that some people were trying to use child sacrifice as a way to worship God. The lesson that God taught Abraham at Mount Moriah had not fully sunk in.

One additional episode of child sacrifice is the cryptic account of a judge, Jephthah, and his daughter. In Judges 11, Jephthah vows to sacrifice whatever or whoever comes out of his house to meet him when he returns if the Lord will help him win a battle. The vow itself doesn't make a whole lot of sense unless you know that some Israelite houses were designed to enclose animals on the first floor and people on the second.[47] An animal or a person could come out of the door. Awfully,

Jephthah's own daughter emerges from the house after his victory in battle, and he feels obligated by his vow to offer her as a sacrifice to the Lord. She accepts her fate and only asks for a little time to mourn her virginity (Jgs 11:37). The text does not clearly state what happens when she comes back, only telling us that Jephthah "did with her according to his vow which he had made" (Jgs 11:39). This incompleteness tempts one to say that he did not actually kill her, but just devoted her to God as a consecrated virgin. But this would be to sidestep the crux of the problem: Jephthah sacrifices his daughter to the Lord as an act of worship and the text of the book does not explicitly judge him for it.

Killing children in religious rituals is an abhorrent practice, and the biblical prophets repeatedly condemn it.

We like clarity, and on some points like this one the Bible is at best ambiguous. However, there are multiple moments in the stories of the patriarchs and judges when a character sins against God and is not directly condemned. The shape of the story reveals the wisdom or folly of his act. In this case, the narrative reveals Jephthah's foolishness. His vow was rash, and he was not morally aware enough to realize that a vow to do something evil is never morally binding. Jephthah makes and fulfills a rash vow. The reader is meant to "get it" and realize that the character is setting a bad example here. Jephthah is only implicitly condemned.

Whether in the story of the Binding of Isaac, the account of Jephthah's daughter, or the many condemnations of Israelites attempting to worship God with child sacrifice, the Bible's message is consistent: child sacrifice is wrong. It is not a legitimate way to worship God. Killing children in religious rituals is an abhorrent practice, and the biblical prophets repeatedly condemn it. Through Jeremiah, God says, "I did not command [it], nor did it come into my mind" (Jer 7:31). The evil practice of child sacrifice is so opposed to what God wants that it doesn't even cross his mind. In fact, from his perspective, "sons are a heritage from the LORD, / the fruit of the womb a reward" (Ps 127:3). Rather than potential victims for a bizarre religious ritual, children are a gift from God meant to be nurtured and celebrated.

Chapter 11

Election: Can God Choose You Instead of Me?

Nobody likes to feel trapped. That's why we hold up opportunity, individualism, and hard work. We embrace the fact that our lives are not predetermined, that our fate is not sealed from the day of our birth. We despise old customs like taking up your father's profession, arranged marriages, inherited money. In the United States especially, we like the story of the underdog, the rags-to-riches millionaire who started with nothing. These stories prove to us that we are not stuck, that there is no glass ceiling, that by our own effort we can change the outcome of our lives. Sometimes this means avoiding the bad habits of our parents, moving to a new place, undoing the harm done to us by others, or just starting over. It's important not to be trapped.

But this is also where we run into trouble with God. As much as we say we like God, we have trouble thinking of him as *really* running the universe as Creator, Judge, and Ruler. We prefer to think of him more like Santa Claus, who gives us toys we like, or even like a space alien who invades earth now and again. The idea that he actually runs the government of the universe, that he built all the structures inherent in the galaxy—gravity, the speed of light, the rotation and orbit of the planets—seems pretty far out to us. Where his government can really bother us is when it rules our behavior and sets up the framework for our existence. We don't like to think of our freedom as being circumscribed by anything, let alone by an all-powerful Being.

God's Choice or My Choice?

Most of the time, though, it is easy for us to think of ourselves in blank terms—or rather, to not think of ourselves. We can get on autopilot and forget that there's a beginning and an end to our lives, that we have a story, a trajectory, a destiny. But when we do get to thinking about things such as destiny and the horizon of our lives, it can be difficult to see how much of our "fate" is in our hands after all. "If I had different circumstances, a different job, a different family, more drive, more talent, then maybe ..." Our freedom, our free will, while in some ways unconditional, is actually hemmed in by many conditions far beyond our control. We cannot choose to be born to different parents, to be a different height, let alone to jump like a frog or swim like a squid. All of these thoughts might seem far from our purpose, but they all point back to this question for a person of faith: "Did God choose me, or did I choose him?" The right answer is "yes, both."

> *It doesn't seem fair to us that God would choose some people and not others. What are we to make of the apparent fact that God elects some and not others?*

The Bible teaches us this principle from multiple angles: "Many are called, but few are chosen" (Mt 22:14). "There is a remnant, chosen by grace" (Rom 11:5). "He destined us in love to be his sons through Jesus Christ, according to the purpose of his will" (Eph 1:5). St. Peter speaks of Christians as "chosen and destined by God the Father" (1 Pt 1:2). If God chooses some for salvation, then what happens to everybody else? Can the chosen ones resist God's will and "unchoose" themselves? It doesn't seem fair to us that God would choose some people and not others. What are we to make of the apparent fact that God elects some and not others?

A Chosen People

The whole problem starts way back in Genesis 12, when God calls Abraham out of Ur to come to the Promised Land and start a new people that will be God's special possession. The line of God's choosing, his "election," continues in the selection of Isaac over Ishmael, Jacob over Esau, and so on. God chooses a particular people, the people of Israel, to demonstrate his love, to reveal his law, and to bring forth his Savior. At first, the notion of God even having a "Chosen People" can startle us—and why Israel? Why didn't he choose the ancient Egyptians or the Chinese or the Romans? While we can't unveil complete answers to these questions, it is clear that God chose a certain people to begin his plan of salvation, to rescue us from our sins. St. Paul explains their unique role: "They are Israelites, and to them belong the sonship, the glory, the covenants, the giving of the law, the worship, and the promises; to them belong the patriarchs, and of their race, according to the flesh, is the Christ. God who is over all be blessed for ever. Amen" (Rom 9:4-5). It might seem like choosing a certain people confines salvation to a select few, but it is actually the reverse. The choosing of the Chosen People opens the way to God for all humanity. From the beginning of God's special call to Abraham, he proclaims that "in you all the families of the earth shall be blessed" (Gn 12:3, NRSV). Abraham is not called by God *instead of* the nations, but *for the sake of* the nations.

God begins teaching the divine pedagogy to a chosen few, in order that his plan of salvation might open up to all. Throughout the history of ancient Israel, God prepares the way for the coming of his Son, who is born a Jew among Jews in order to save all, both Jew and Gentile. Jesus even says very clearly, "Salvation is from the Jews" (Jn 4:22). He comes to deliver on that promise. The Jews retain a unique status as God's Chosen People and our "elder brothers in the faith," but now the plan of salvation is opened up in Christ so that Gentiles might too become "heirs according to promise" (Gal 3:29) and be "grafted in" (Rom 11:17) to the natural family of God. We can enter his people and become members of the new "Israel of God" (Gal 6:16) through faith in Christ and the sacraments of initiation: baptism, confirmation, and the Eucharist. Election is essential to the divine pedagogy. It shows us who God is, how he wants us to live, and what his plan is. It prepares the way for Christ and opens a new path of "blessing for all nations."

Predestination

Now if God chose a certain people at a certain time in history to receive his revelation, that's one matter, but our eternal destiny is another. God chose Israel, but does he choose each person who gets saved? Yes. This principle, that God chooses or elects all those who will be saved, is called the doctrine of predestination. St. Paul expresses this teaching while reflecting on the Old Testament:

> For he says to Moses, "I will have mercy on whom I have mercy, and I will have compassion on whom I have compassion." So it depends not upon man's will or exertion, but upon God's mercy. For the scripture says to Pharaoh, "I have raised you up for the very purpose of showing my power in you, so that my name may be proclaimed in all the earth." So then he has mercy upon whomever he wills, and he hardens the heart of whomever he wills. (Rom 9:15-18)

This means we can't earn mercy; we only receive it as a gift. We can respond to God's invitation in faith, but even our very faith is a gift in itself. God chooses or elects the saved, but not against their will. He doesn't force anyone to go to heaven. Catholic teaching holds to predestination, that God knows and intends for all eternity the salvation of the saved, but that he predestines no one for hell. (This is different from some Protestant forms of predestination, which claim that God does predestine some people for hell—sometimes called the theory of "double predestination.") God is not coercing people to do what he wants, but electing, choosing, and giving grace to the saved. He truly has mercy on whom he wills. Those who reject God, who willfully turn away from him, get what they want: eternal separation from him in hell.[48] God does not create souls merely to damn them—that would be sadistic. Instead, he allows us either to choose him in love or to reject him in hate. He respects the choice we make.

God gives everyone the grace they need to turn to him, but not all will respond, not all will persevere.

So he chooses us, but we also choose him. St. Paul cites a passage from Malachi to prove his point about predestination: "Jacob I loved, but Esau I hated" (Rom 9:13, quoting Mal 1:2-3). The original context of the prophecy is about the divine judgments, which God has brought upon Esau's descendants, but St. Paul uses it as an illustration of divine election. God chose one people, but not another. The idea of God "hating" anyone sounds crazy, but it matches the same kind of language which expresses a strong choice that Jesus uses when he says, "If any one comes to me and does not hate his own father and mother and wife and children and brothers and sisters, yes, and even his own life, he cannot be my disciple" (Lk 14:26). Jesus does not want us to intend evil toward our family members, but he does want to choose God as our first priority, to love him the most. God gives everyone the grace they need to turn to him, but not all will respond, not all will persevere. Even those who initially respond can lose salvation through mortal sin. God elects or predestines the saved from all eternity to join him in heaven, in concert with, not in contradiction to, our own wills.

Catholic theologians also talk about different stages in the process of election. A person is called by God, then led by grace to respond to him. Then a person is "justified," meaning that he or she enters into a state of grace, normally by faith and baptism. Finally, an elect person receives the grace of "final perseverance," the grace to remain faithful to God till the end, to die in a state of grace and enter into God's presence in heaven. St. Paul tightly summarizes how this works: "For those whom he foreknew he also predestined to be conformed to the image of his Son, in order that he might be the first-born among many brethren. And those whom he predestined he also called; and those whom he called he also justified; and those whom he justified he also glorified" (Rom 8:29-30). It might seem unfair that God chooses some and not others, but if the whole project of salvation rested solely with us, if I could get myself to heaven merely by my own choices, then salvation would be a human work instead of a divine one. The doctrine of predestination shows us that God is the one who saves. He does not just invite us, but empowers us to respond to him. His grace prompts every little act of our will that tends toward him in the first place. His love draws us, helps us, and aids us along the way to his presence in heaven. And yes, God can choose you instead of me, but I hope he chooses both of us!

Chapter 12

Innocent Suffering

"Why, God?"

That's a question we like to ask when things go wrong, especially when they go *way* wrong. If, apparently for no reason, something bad happens to us or to someone we love, we feel deep inside that it is not fair. Bad things shouldn't happen to good people. Innocent people shouldn't suffer. The question arises in millions of gut-wrenching scenarios: It's not fair that some people are born into the lap of luxury, while others are born in the slums of Haiti. It is not fair that many children die of terminal illnesses, while many others develop into healthy adults. Hurricanes and tornadoes strike randomly, unfairly. There is no logic, no reasoning, no explanation that will make the pain of these situations go away. When someone dies in an accident or a terrorist attack or from a disease, we can't ignore the pain, the loss, the sorrow of it.

The pain of suffering has prompted many people to shake their fists at God, to shout at him, to complain that in his all-powerful might he did nothing to stop the evil from coming, did nothing to fix it once it came. The Bible gives us an example of this kind of pain in the Book of Job. Job is "blameless and upright" (Jb 1:1), but God allows him to suffer terrible loss. His children die in a storm. His servants are killed. His wealth is plundered. His body is covered with sores. In his plight, his wife advises him, "Curse God and die" (Jb 2:9), but Job remains stubbornly faithful to the Lord. In the midst of his suffering, he seeks an answer to the problem.

God's Power and Goodness

The problem of suffering boils down to a showdown between God's goodness and his power. If God were good but not all-powerful, we wouldn't be too bothered. He would just be smaller than the evil in the world, but that would be evil in itself—to have an evil force bigger than God. If God were all-powerful, but not all-good, then he would sometimes use his power to do arbitrary or evil things, which would be bad. So if God is both all-good and all-powerful, we have a problem. It seems as if he should put a stop to any and every evil, injustice, and innocent suffering right now. But we know that many injustices persist, many innocent people die, many bad things happen to good people. What are we to make of this inexplicable reality?

> *So if God is both all-good and all-powerful, we have a problem. It seems as if he should put a stop to any and every evil, injustice, and innocent suffering right now.*

Some suffering is caused by people. Wars, terrorism, human-caused accidents, and crimes can be explained as human problems, the results of human evil or human error. Bad people do bad things, and sometimes good people suffer as a result. We can lay our petition of complaint at the feet of human beings who are directly responsible. God is only indirectly the cause of these problems since he created free human beings in the first place. He does not prompt evil people to do evil things, but he does not prevent them from doing evil things either. He does not violate human freedom, which would be evil in itself, to prevent all evil consequences. If God were to restrain people from committing all evils, then we would not really be free. We would be trapped, programmed like robots to obey God. We could not choose for the good since there would be no evil choices to reject. While many disasters could be averted and we could never experience hate, we would never be able to love.

The ultimate test case for God's power and goodness is natural disaster, or what we could even call "natural evil." If children die in an earthquake or a tornado, we have no human beings to blame. In this case, God not only does not prevent the evil, but actually seems to cause it by allowing natural occurrences such as earthquakes and tornadoes. He created them; innocent people were killed. God is either not all-good or not all-loving, so the logic goes. If we don't get this far down the path of reasoning, we at least ask why. Why do tornadoes kill people? Why does God not only allow that, but seemingly plan for it?

There are two directions from which we can begin to think about this conundrum. The first begins with God's wise ordering and creation of the universe. He made the world good, but included in that goodness are natural laws such as gravity, weather patterns, and the movements of the earth's crust. These natural laws undergird the good world which we inhabit but also have a cost. Trees get struck by lightning, rivers flood, people age, the earth quakes. The natural processes which unfold according to the wise design of God can seem chaotic and do cause suffering, but it is worth considering how much more chaotic the world would be if God constantly intervened in the laws of his own creation to hold back the flood waters or cause gravity to work backward. In addition, many natural disasters could be averted by not building in flood plains or along fault lines, or by taking simple precautions such as washing our hands and cutting down trees near our homes. A creation that did not proceed according to fixed and universal laws would be messy, random, and unpredictable in a way that would limit the value of human freedom. We wouldn't be able to take precautions to keep ourselves safe.

On the other hand, we can look to the theology of sin. The original sin of Adam and Eve damages creation, unleashing a Pandora's box of evil consequences, and breaks man's original "harmony with creation."[49] Before their sin, Adam and Eve were not subject to death, so they would not have suffered from the natural evils that we do, but afterward "creation was subjected to futility" (Rom 8:20), including the inevitability of death. From these two directions we can navigate toward answering those burning questions about how on earth God could allow such evils.

Retribution

When we demand explanations from God for our suffering, what is it we're really asking for? Justice. We want good people to get good things out of life and bad people to reap bad things. We have a nose for justice and don't like it when we smell a rat. If a criminal becomes wealthy and gets away with all his crimes, we sense the injustice of it. If an honest person is falsely accused and falsely imprisoned, we feel the evil of it deep in our gut. We long for what is called *retribution*. Retribution is all about getting your just deserts, getting what you deserve for what you've done. We like that idea.

In Old Testament times, people felt the same way. "An eye for an eye, a tooth for a tooth" (see Ex 21:24; Mt 5:38) was their way of expressing the desire for justice. It meant your punishment couldn't be disproportionate. You couldn't get the death penalty for stealing a loaf of bread. The definitive form of retribution thinking is *divine* retribution, where the all-powerful God is the one responsible for dishing out just deserts.

This theory of divine retribution appears many times in the Bible. "Vengeance is mine," says the Lord (Dt 32:35). Those who follow the path of wisdom and keep the law of God are promised blessing, life, prosperity, descendants, even land (Dt 28:1-14). However, the flip side is also true: Those who walk the path of folly, reject God and fail to keep his commandments, will bring down his wrath and curses on their heads (Dt 28:15-68). This general principle of divine retribution is established early on in the Bible. We see examples of God's wrath in the Flood, the Tower of Babel, the plagues of Egypt, and the golden calf episode, but also examples of God's blessing on Abraham, Isaac, Jacob, Joseph, Moses, and Joshua. Even the Psalms and Proverbs hold up the idea of divine retribution as a crucial motivator for living the good life. The basic idea is very simple: keeping the commandments leads to life and blessing, while breaking the commandments leads to death and curse.

The trouble is, life has a way of being backward. For example, while it is generally true that if you work hard, save your money, pay your taxes, and participate in your community, you're more likely to have a prosperous and happy future. However, in some cases a person "does everything right" but is cheated out of their money by an unscrupulous person (like Bernie Madoff), is overcome by a terminal illness, or is irreparably harmed in an accident. Life does not always deliver perfect justice. The Bible raises this problem several times, as when Ecclesiastes offers this poignant observation:

> There is an evil which I have seen under the sun, and it lies heavy upon men: a man to whom God gives wealth, possessions, and honor, so that he lacks nothing of all that he desires, yet God does not give him power to enjoy them, but a stranger enjoys them; this is vanity; it is a sore affliction. (Eccl 6:1-2)

Ecclesiastes sees how upside down the world can be—what should be is not, and what should not be is. People do not always receive what is due to them. Returning to Job, we see a "blameless and upright" man who is afflicted with every suffering conceivable: his children die, his wealth perishes, his body is afflicted with sores. All of this evil comes upon him without provocation. He did nothing wrong and yet suffered greatly. As St. John Paul II teaches, "While it is true that suffering has a meaning as punishment, when it is connected with a fault, *it is not true* that *all suffering is a consequence of a fault and has the nature of punishment.*"[50] Job's suffering was not a punishment. Rather, Job's suffering is mysterious, functioning as a test of his fidelity to the Lord, not as a punishment for wrongdoing. Job asks God a million questions about his fate, mulling over and over again how these evils could have come upon him. But he does not receive answers to his many questions. Rather, God simply arrives on the scene. Job puts his hand over his mouth (Jb 40:3-5) and repents for questioning the wisdom of God (Jb 42:1-6).

> *We can't figure out exactly how God's calculus of justice works, but the main secret ingredient is time. God gives the wicked time to repent.*

If the Bible presents us with an ideal picture of obedience and blessing versus disobedience and curse, then how does the story of Job and his rubber-meeting-the-road example help modify what it is teaching? The answer is painfully simple, yet profoundly important: time. Time is the game-changer. Divine retribution is a true doctrine. God is all-powerful and all-just. He will deliver everyone's just deserts to them eventually. However, often the Old Testament era perspectives were exclusively focused on the here and now. The ancients wanted to see God's justice for all here on earth, right away, on time, with no delay. We would all like that, maybe. The Book of Job does not trash divine-retribution theology but adds a layer of complexity. We can't figure out exactly how God's calculus of justice works, but the main secret ingredient is time. God gives the wicked time to repent (Rom 2:4; Rv 2:21). In the end, at what we often call the Final Judgment, God will judge everyone and everything. He will right every wrong, punish every evil, and undo the horrible knots of sin.

Again, that might seem unfair. The suffering heart cries out: "I don't want to wait. I am suffering *now*. I want justice *now*." But before we plead with God to dish out divine justice right away, every time, we might want to pause and consider how this delay of justice fits in with divine wisdom.

Sin and Suffering

We like to talk about "innocent people" or "good people" as those who suffer unjustly. But when we use words like "innocent," we mean "innocent in a certain respect"—that is, "they didn't do anything to deserve *that*." This might seem like nit-picking, but it's crucial to the theological truth at stake here. We don't mean that the person is universally innocent, totally perfect, sinless, and has never done anything wrong. If we reflect back on our earlier discussion of death, then we should recall the biblical teaching that "the wages of sin is death" (Rom 6:23). All death is a result of sin.[51] All sin orients us toward death. Since we all inherit original sin, we are destined for death from the moment of our birth. Death is inescapable because of sin. Ultimately, this insight points to another principle in Paul's Letter to the Romans: no one is righteous. He quotes Psalm 14 to prove his point: "None is righteous, no, not one; no one understands, no one seeks for God. All have turned aside, together they have gone wrong; no one does good, not even one" (Rom 3:10-12). His point is that "all have sinned and fall short of the glory of God" (Rom 3:23). We don't deserve God. We don't deserve peace. We don't deserve eternal life. For us to suffer or even for our lives to be cut short by tornadoes or terrorists, we should not be astonished.

Now, that is not to say that someone who suffers from a tsunami or an earthquake brought it upon himself or deserved it. It is very dangerous for us to play God and judge people when bad things happen to others. Jesus himself rejects attempts to blame people for the evils they suffer from

(Lk 13:1-5; Jn 9:1-3). The right response involves sympathy, disaster relief, aid to those who are in need, and a realization that the disaster could have just as easily happened to us. In fact, we all suffer from the consequences of a broken world and are guaranteed to partake of the suffering of death. While there are a handful of biblical examples of divinely caused natural disasters, such as the plagues in Egypt, most natural disasters remain beyond our ability to fully explain. We know that God is good and creates a good world that functions according to good natural laws, so building a house in a flood plain and constructing a skyscraper with a shallow foundation are bound to be bad ideas. God does not routinely invade his creation to violate the laws of nature, but we know that he does actively work against evil and suffering. In the Bible, we see him saving, redeeming, healing, rescuing, and binding up the brokenhearted. We also know that somehow creation itself is wounded by human sin. Scripture says it is "subjected to futility" (Rom 8:20), that it is in "bondage to decay" (Rom 8:21), and that it is "groaning in travail" (Rom 8:22) for redemption. But the lines of responsibility are not easy to draw. Exactly how human sin is linked to natural evils is blurry and mysterious, and we know that God is actively working to destroy evil and bring about the redemption of the human race. We are in the middle of the story and will not see his final victory until the end. In the meantime, often the true answer to suffering is sympathy, tears, and even crying out to God, rather than philosophical problem-solving.

Humanity as a whole has brought evil and death upon itself. We can blame Adam and Eve, Osama bin Laden, or our next-door neighbor, but the reality of suffering flows from the reality of human sin. No one is righteous, and so no one is exempt from suffering. All of us born under sin are on the wide path of destruction (Mt 7:13), subject to the wrath of God (Rom 1:18), and in need of redemption. This is why Jesus preaches a message of repentance. We need to turn away from sin and turn toward God in order to get off the path to destruction. Hell, separation from God, is the natural path for those who are born in sin and then choose to sin. Sin leads away from God.

Okay, so sin rules over the sinner and we're all sinners, so we deserve death and destruction. But if God is both all-good and all-powerful, then why do evil and suffering exist in the first place?

In the same way that darkness is a privation of light, evil only "exists" as an absence of good.

Here's where things get weird. Evil doesn't exist, at least not as a true substance. That might sound like crazy talk, but let me explain. Evil is like a hole. A hole in a shirt or in the dirt doesn't exist as a thing, so to speak. Instead, it "exists" as the absence of a thing—the absence of fabric or dirt. This is what evil is like. Theologians call it a *privation* of good. In the same way that darkness is a privation of light, evil only "exists" as an absence of good. So God does not create evil, but rather people who make evil choices choose against good, against Being, against God. God allows evils to invade his good created order, but he finds a way to bring good out of evil. He does not allow evil to overwhelm the good. In fact, he even enters into our plight of suffering. Jesus did not live in a palace but walked the streets with us. He did not eschew the difficulties of human life but endured terrible sufferings for our sake in order that the power of evil might be broken. By suffering himself, Jesus redeems suffering. It is no longer meaningless, but salvific. When we suffer, we can participate in his sufferings and our pains are transformed into beautiful contributions to the redemption of creation.[52] While we cannot definitively crack the nut of the mystery of human suffering, our very shock at the injustice of suffering originates from God, who embodies the standard of good and evil. If God did not exist, then our outrage would have no moral foundation; we just would find ourselves not *liking* the suffering we see, and evil would actually win. Though we do not understand why God delays fixing the whole universe, our reaction to suffering proves to be a meaningful, divinely derived, compassionate response to the world around us. We should reel in horror and reach out in sympathy when others suffer, but we should remember that God is on our side in the battle against suffering and evil. He even suffered with us to join in our cause, and we can be confident that at the end of the story, good will triumph.

Of course, we could write a thousand books about suffering and evil, but the principles for understanding all the complex arguments that philosophers, theologians, and others make boil down to a few simple concepts. God is all-good and all-powerful. Evil is a privation of good. No one is righteous. All are born under sin and are therefore subject to death. God does bring justice, but we might have to wait until the end of time for all of the loose ends to be tied together. In fact, God walks with us on the path of suffering, suffers on our behalf, and fights on our side against the evil in the world. Deep down we know the unjust and terrible sufferings so many people undergo are simply not right. There's no way to stare a suffering person in the face and simply explain away his or her troubles. But we can trust that when he returns, God will judge everyone everywhere and undo the wrongs and injustices of this world. Someday, "he will wipe away every tear" (Rv 21:4), and our hearts will finally rest in the victory of God's justice.

Chapter 13

Polygamy, Incest, and Divorce

Certain things about the Old Testament strike us as just plain weird. Here's our chance to sort through the weirdness and see what we can find. In particular, I want to examine polygamy, incest, and divorce. Having multiple wives seems bizarre to us, something for humorous operas such as Mozart's *The Abduction from the Seraglio* or a thing to be mocked in silly stories such as "The Butterfly That Stamped," by Rudyard Kipling. The practice is forbidden by our civil law, but it was not that long ago that Mormons revived the Old Testament custom of polygamy. And even today, a handful of Muslims retain the practice. Incest, the marrying of a close relative, is even more revolting, and criminal, yet it appears several times in the Bible. Divorce and remarriage are permitted in the Old Testament, but not in the New. Why is that? We'll take on each of these issues in turn.

Polygamy

Many of our favorite Old Testament heroes were polygamists: Abraham, Jacob, David, Solomon. These figures took not only multiple wives but concubines as well. These are not insignificant characters who get a mere footnote in the Old Testament; they are essential parts of the story, crucial links in the chain of salvation history. Even the offspring from their polygamous relationships are indispensable. The twelve sons of Jacob, who are the namesakes for the twelve tribes of Israel, were born of four different women, two wives and two concubines (Gn 29:31—30:24). While the Bible doesn't tell us exactly how many wives David had, we have the names of eight of them,[53] and we know he left behind ten concubines to care for his palace when he fled (2 Sm 15:16), so that makes at least eighteen consorts. Plus, we are told he took an unspecified number of additional wives and concubines (2 Sm 5:13), bringing the total to at least twenty-four. Solomon, of course, is famous for having seven hundred wives and three hundred concubines (1 Kgs 11:3), but even if this number is an exaggeration, the Song of Songs indicates he had "sixty queens and eighty concubines and virgins without number" (Song 6:8, ESV). Either way, Solomon's wife-count is extraordinary and dwarfs Abraham's choice to take one wife (perhaps two[54]) and one concubine (or perhaps more[55]). All these wives and concubines raise a few questions for us.

> *This shows the divine pedagogy at work. God first restricts polygamy, then eventually abolishes it, as he slowly turns up the light of revelation.*

We know instinctively that polygamy is wrong, but why exactly? The answer to this question might help us sort through the evidence. In fact, the Bible itself, while narrating the stories of the ancient kings and patriarchs, censures the practice repeatedly. From the beginning, God created one man and one woman in the Garden of Eden. He did not create two or four or a thousand wives for Adam, but just one, in order to show his design for the human family. From the beginning monogamous marriage is held up as the ideal (Gn 2:18, 24). St. Augustine comments on this early stage of revelation: "That the good purpose of marriage, however, is better promoted by one husband with one wife, than by a husband with several wives, is shown plainly enough by the very first union of a married pair, which was made by the Divine Being Himself, with the intention of marriages taking their beginning therefrom, and of its affording to them a more honourable precedent."[56] Polygamy was not part of God's design.

The biblical narrative reaffirms this fact repeatedly. When the childless Abraham takes matters into his own hands and lies with Hagar, his wife's servant, the project backfires. Abraham and Hagar's son, Ishmael, does not become the child of promise, but his birth introduces chaos into Abraham's household (Gn 16:5; 21:10). Hagar and Ishmael are eventually banished from the family with God's approval (Gn 21:12). Abraham's polygamous actions are not rewarded, but thwarted. While early on the Bible does not ban polygamy, it places limits and restrictions on the practice. It demands that every wife be treated equally (Ex 21:10) and that the children of each wife have their inheritance rights respected (Dt 21:15-17). Even the king "shall not multiply wives for himself" (Dt 17:17). This shows the divine pedagogy at work. God first restricts polygamy, then eventually abolishes it, as he slowly turns up the light of revelation.

Very early on, the Bible shows the violent, twisted results that polygamy can produce. The first polygamist, Lamech, is described as a bloodthirsty man (Gn 4:19,23-24). His sexual choice to dominate others leads him along a violent path. King David's polygamy, which contradicts the rule of Deuteronomy, leads him to lust, power-rape, and murder in the case of Bathsheba and her husband (2 Sm 11). Then, after his personal sins, his sons are provoked to similar behaviors: Amnon rapes his half-sister Tamar (2 Sm 13); Absalom murders him and launches a rebellion (2 Sm 13-16). Eventually, Absalom's revolt finds him ravishing David's concubines on the palace rooftop (2 Sm 16:22). David's sexual behaviors unleash a hornets' nest of sin. Even his favored son, Solomon, who imitates and expands David's polygamy, is in the end led astray by his hundreds of wives and concubines to worship false gods (1 Kgs 11:4). Polygamy does not end well for those who practice it in the biblical story.

In the New Testament, polygamy is implicitly condemned. Jesus talks of a husband and wife becoming "one flesh" in marital union (Mt 19:5). Several times, the New Testament mandates that early Christian clergymen be "the husband of one wife" (1 Tm 3:2, 12; Ti 1:6). From the beginning, the Church has banned polygamy, as it is against the nature of marriage as God designed it. According to St. John Paul II, polygamy "directly negates the plan of God which was revealed from the beginning, because it is contrary to the equal personal dignity of men and women who in matrimony give themselves with a love that is total and therefore unique and exclusive."[57] Polygamy is misogynistic. It disrespects women by treating them like property and clouds the reality that men and woman are equal in dignity before God. The Bible tells us about the polygamous practices of the ancients, but it also legally restricts the practice, shows us its horrible consequences, and eventually bans it altogether.

Incest

When people start reading the Bible, they find Adam and Eve in the Garden, but soon after they begin to ask: "Wait a second! If Adam and Eve were the *only humans*, then where did their children get spouses from? Where did Cain's wife come from?" It is a logical question. We know incest—the marrying of family members—is wrong on both a moral and biological level. Inbreeding can cause serious genetic problems. But if there were only two humans, then incest seems unavoidable. It is a conundrum.

Three considerations will help us get our minds around this. First, if God had specially created multiple individuals to be the spouses of Adam and Eve, then there would be more than one human family, more than one human race. Individually created persons would not be united with one another by blood or marriage. There would be multiple original couples and the human family would be divided from the get-go. Clearly, that kind of division was opposed to God's design. He wanted all of us to be part of the same family.[58] Racist writers in the past wanted to divide people into different groups based on what kinds of apes they evolved from, but even secular science has shown that all of us are related, that there is only one human race. All human beings share genetic data. We are all part of the same family. Second, we can speculate that if the children of Adam and Eve married one another, a few problems would arise on the biological level. Normally, inbreeding causes genetic problems that can result in congenital birth defects or early death, but if Adam and Eve were the first human beings, their genetic code would be flawless. The genetic mutations that cause problems over a span of generations would not arise so early in the history of our race. Third, early in Genesis, the practice of incest was not yet forbidden. The laws against incest are in Leviticus 18, which was written long after our first human ancestors roamed the earth. As is apparent in the story of Lot and his daughters (Gn 19:30-38), Genesis clearly forbids sexual relations between parent and child, but not in certain other family relations. For example, Abraham himself married his half-sister, Sarah (Gn 20:12). Indeed, often in the ancient Near East, royal persons would marry their relatives to consolidate power in a single family, and the biblical characters abide by similar customs.

Eventually, God's law forbids the practice of marrying one's close relatives (Lv 18). This proscription demonstrates again the gradualism of God's teaching strategy. He wants all of us to be one family, so we are descended from common parents, meaning that siblings and other close relatives married early in the history of humanity. But once the family tree was large enough, the Lord forbade marrying close relatives. The *Catechism* teaches that "incest corrupts family relationships and marks a regression toward animality" (2388). And even animals tend to avoid mating with close relatives. Incest represents a step backward, a corruption, a blurring of the lines in relationships. While intermarriage of relatives was essential in the early formation of the human race, now it is strictly forbidden. In Catholic practice, canon law regulates exactly how closely spouses can be related.[59] Parent-child, brother-sister, first cousin-first cousin, uncle-niece marriages are all banned. In rare circumstances, a bishop can grant a dispensation to let two first cousins, but not closer relatives, marry. Civil laws often also put limits on how closely marriage partners can be related.

> *While intermarriage of relatives was essential in the early formation of the human race, now it is strictly forbidden.*

Divorce

Divorce is ugly, but common. About fifty percent of U.S. marriages end in divorce. In the Bible, divorce is permitted in the Old Testament but prohibited in the New. The old law lays out certain rules governing divorce and remarriage (Dt 24:1-4), permitting it under certain circumstances. But Jesus specifically mentions, "For your hardness of heart Moses allowed you to divorce your wives, but from the beginning it was not so" (Mt 19:8). Jesus cites the earlier precedent of Adam and Eve, whose marriage was a lifelong monogamous covenant, not a temporary relationship that could be dissolved. He overturns the Old Testament precedent, which was only a concession, and reintroduces God's original plan for marriage. The Church holds fast to Jesus' teaching on divorce. The *Catechism* clearly states, "Divorce is a grave offense against the natural law" (2384). The practice purports to break the unbreakable bond of marriage. Even though the Church permits civil divorce and separation in some circumstances, the marriage itself remains indissoluble.[60] Remarriage after divorce is the real problem. Jesus says, "Whoever divorces his wife, except for unchastity [Greek *porneia*], and marries another, commits adultery" (Mt 19:9). Remarrying after a divorce is therefore equivalent to adultery. Or, in another way, it could been seen as a kind of serial monogamy, which is really polygamy—a marriage to multiple partners over time. The exception Jesus mentions, *porneia*, is best interpreted as marriage to a close relative, an incestuous, invalid marriage that should be annulled. The *Catechism* calls the state of remarriage after divorce "public and permanent adultery."[61]

The biblical history of polygamy, incest, and divorce show us again the way that God goes about teaching us. He does not blast humanity with hard teachings all at once but slowly enlightens his children over time. Lifelong monogamous marriage was God's plan for Adam and Eve. While it was necessary for their children to intermarry for the spread of the human race according to God's command (Gn 1:28), eventually marriage to relatives was forbidden by his law. Polygamy was never part of the plan, but when it crept in, God's law restricted it, discouraged it, and eventually abolished it. Divorce and remarriage followed a similar trajectory. Jesus teaches that marriage is indissoluble until death. Polygamy, incest, and remarriage after divorce are violations of God's law. They do not do justice to God's plan for the human family, to the equal dignity of spouses, or to the beautifully unbreakable bond of marriage.

Chapter 14

Does God Approve of Slavery, Misogyny, and Other Evils?

The Bible makes us bristle. It records so many evil practices as it tells the story of salvation. We've already seen what the Bible has to say about child sacrifice, polygamy, killing, and other troublesome customs, but other things in the story are societal structures that are alien to us and objectively immoral. Often it seems as if biblical writers are "giving a pass" to the people who engage in things such as slavery and misogyny, and bizarre behavior such as mutilation, nudism, and deception. Volumes have been written about these topics and many more will be written, so we can't solve everything in just one chapter. But I do hope to show you a few interpretational "tacks" worth considering to sort through what sometimes looks like a horror show of immoralities.

First, we should recognize that when we read the Bible as God's Word, we are always dealing with at least two contexts—one is what God wants; the other is what human cultures want. God, as the Supreme Being and Creator, intervenes in history by revealing himself, his power, his truth, his ways to human beings. However, the trouble is that he finds us wrapped up in our own circumstances, issues, and problems. Effectively changing us stubborn human beings takes time and finesse. God invests a lot of energy into teaching and reshaping humanity to be more like him, but it takes a long time.

Here we go back to the principle of the divine pedagogy: God reveals himself to humanity gradually. Concretely, that means that he encounters human beings in an ancient Near Eastern culture with its own customs, circumstances, proclivities, limitations, and imperfections. Rather than expecting perfection from them all at once, he helps them step-by-step to come to grips with his plan for humanity. God is not compromising the truth, but he is accommodating weak and troubled people, teaching them by slowly altering their perspective in limiting, restricting, and eventually eradicating immoral cultural practices.

> *When we read the Bible as God's Word, we are always dealing with at least two contexts—one is what God wants; the other is what human cultures want.*

Slavery

The first immoral practice we'll examine is slavery. Slavery "is a sin against the dignity of persons and their fundamental rights."[62] It reduces people to objects or tools to be used by those who "own" them. Slavery is an injustice, an outrage, a moral horror that deceives regarding the beauty, dignity, and true worth of human beings. People cannot, in truth, be bought or sold. People cannot truly be possessions or property. Slavery is a lie. But we find many slaves in the Bible. Several biblical characters are slaves—the centurion's slave, the high priest's slave. Biblical heroes such as Abraham had slaves. In fact, the whole nation of Israel was enslaved in Egypt for generations. Slaves appear in the Ten Commandments and other biblical laws. Even the New Testament gives teachings specifically to slaves. Nowhere in the Bible do we find and explicit, wholehearted repudiation of the institution of slavery. But today's Church teaching is clearly opposed to slavery, so what are we to make of all of the biblical accounts of slavery?

Slavery was part of the cultural fabric of the ancient Near East. Slaves made up almost half the population in many places and performed a variety of tasks from the nasty work of the mines to overseeing the household affairs of the wealthy, a very different social situation from the severe racially based mode of slavery in the American South before the Civil War. While slaves were the least free of all people, many other people had their freedom severely restricted by their economic status as serfs or indentured servants who worked rented land. You could become a slave by being captured as a prisoner of war, by selling yourself willingly (or unwillingly) to pay off your debts, or by being sold by your family. You could also be born into slavery. Most slaves became household servants, as we see in biblical characters such as Hagar, Sarah's slave, or Joseph, Potiphar's slave.

The slavery laws of the Old Testament begin to shine a light in this dark corner of the ancient world, slowly but surely revealing the fact that God's plan for humanity does not include owning people as if they were cattle.

The Old Law does not explicitly approve or disapprove of slavery, but it does limit its severity. Slaves could marry free persons (1 Chr 2:34-35). Slaves were to be circumcised and participate in the household worship (Ex 12:44)—for example, they could not be forced to work on the Sabbath (Ex 20:8). While they are categorized as property (Ex 20:17), they could also own property. Sometimes, slaves could even own slaves (2 Sm 19:17). Unlike other ancient law codes, biblical law provides for the punishment of a master who murders his own slave (Ex 21:20). Indeed, if a slave owner even knocked out a slave's tooth, he was required to set him free (Ex 21:26-27).

Sometimes slaves were able to raise enough money to purchase their freedom (Lv 25:47-50). Surprisingly, if a free person found a fugitive slave seeking asylum, *he was forbidden to hand him over to his master* (Dt 23:15-16). Hebrew slaves were supposed to be released in the periodic jubilee year (Lv 25:54-55). These examples demonstrate that the Mosaic law restricted the extent and harshness of slavery, even providing slaves with access to justice and means of worship. While the laws still envision slavery as part of the warp and woof of society, they are notably less harsh than other ancient law codes with regard to slaves.

The slavery laws of the Old Testament begin to shine a light in this dark corner of the ancient world, slowly but surely revealing the fact that God's plan for humanity does not include owning people as if they were cattle. Recognizing the humanity of slaves by not allowing them to be abused and by allowing them to participate in the social and religious life of free people is a step in the right direction, toward fully embracing their human dignity.

In the New Testament, we don't encounter many slaves in the Jewish world of first-century Palestine, but there are quite a few slaves in the wider Greco-Roman world to which the apostles bring the Gospel message. Wealthy households normally had slaves who would be responsible for cooking, cleaning, and even tutoring. Slaves were often released from service as they got older or at the death of their master, who included their manumission in his will. Early converts to Christianity often came in household groups, where everyone from the head of the household down to the lowest slave would all be baptized together (Acts 16:15; 18:8; 1 Cor 1:16). This created an odd experience, where both master and slave would worship together as Christians—"slaves or free" (1 Cor 12:13). The message of the Gospel thus had a leveling effect such that those who were normally separated in status would be united as believers in Christ. Yet the institution of slavery still existed, so we find St. Paul, for example, encouraging both slaves and masters to exercise their secular roles in a Christ-like manner (Eph 6:5-9; Col 3:22—4:1). However, St. Paul also encourages slaves to seek their freedom (1 Cor 7:21) and in one extraordinary case he sends an escaped slave back to his master with a weighty endorsement, to receive him "no longer as a slave but more than a slave, as a beloved brother" (Phlm 1:16). Paul also uses slavery as a metaphor for sin (Rom 6:16-22).

The New Testament does not take slavery head-on in a cultural showdown, but it does plant the seeds of freedom by pointing to our equality in Christ and by suggesting that slaves be set free, and even by showing that Jesus comes to deliver the true jubilee year, which includes setting slaves free (Lk 4:18). Eventually, the Roman slavery system would break down with the rest of the empire, and slavery would die a slow death, driven in part by the teaching of the New Testament. Again, we see how God gradually reveals his teaching by first restricting, then humanizing, then eventually eliminating an evil cultural practice.

Misogyny

The treatment of women in the Bible prompts many to accuse the text of misogyny, of hating women. Yet, as we saw with the Bible's approach to slavery, things are not always as they seem. It would take a long book to dig through every important text on women in detail, but here I would like to examine a few details to make broader suggestions about how to understand the Bible's approach to women.

First, the discussion is often cast in terms of power. Women in the Bible appear in traditional cultures where the family, not the individual, is the basic unit of society. The biblical world, in both the Old and New Testaments, was shaped by patriarchal cultures which modern feminism accuses of being "androcentric." Whether we're talking about the nomadic patriarchs of pastoral cultures in the ancient Near East or the *pater familias* of the Roman Empire, ancient cultures emphasized the family as a group with the father at the head of the family. In the best circumstances, this system was "family-centric" rather than "androcentric." Yes, this situation did often create an unfair advantage for men, but it did not leave women powerless. In fact, the Bible tells many stories of women who found a way to use the present patriarchal system in a powerful way—some for good (Ruth, Esther, the daughters of Zelophehad) and some for ill (Athaliah, Jezebel, the wife of Herod). Rather than smashing the ancient cultures' understanding of women at the beginning, God chooses to slowly reveal his plan over time. Polygamy, for example, is a twisted form of patriarchalism, but the Bible is skeptical of it, limits it, and eventually suppresses it. Power as we think of it is usually individualistic, but in a family-based society, power was distributed and used on a group basis, and the groups—families, clans, tribes—were led by men. Good leaders, whether men or women, don't use their power to oppress people, but to help individuals cooperate with one another. The Bible places limits on the power of individuals in order that we might work together to submit ourselves to the power of God.

> *While the Ten Commandments warn that wives might be coveted (Ex 20:17), they declare that mothers are to be honored.*

Second, the legal setup of the Old Testament is often criticized as seeing women as property rather than as persons. For example, wives, but not husbands, are included in the Ten Commandments' list of items that should not be coveted (Ex 20:17). Also, some find the law proposes a "bride price" for women and requires a widow to marry her deceased husband's brother if she has not produced a male heir, what is called "levirate marriage" (Dt 25:5-10). Women can be tried for adultery in a strange ceremony based solely on their husband's "spirit of jealousy" (Nm 5). Even some of the ritual laws appear inequitable, as when a mother who gives birth to a daughter is considered "unclean" for a longer period than a mother who gives birth to a son (Lv 12:1-8).

What are we to make of all of these seemingly unfair rules? If we go back to the idea of the family as the basic unit of society and take into account some other biblical evidence, these oddities start to fall into place. The old law takes human reproduction very seriously. Children are the future, and therefore many of these laws try to protect the central role that women play in the continuance of the family. While the Ten Commandments warn that wives might be coveted (Ex 20:17), they declare that mothers are to be honored (20:12). In fact, the Old Testament repeatedly emphasizes honoring one's mother and her wise teachings (Prv 30:17; Sir 3:4).

The "bride price" (*mohar*) concept originates from passages that mention money given by the groom-to-be to the father of the bride (Gn 34:12; 1 Sm 18:25; Ex 22:16). This exchange of money should not be thought of as a purchase, but a cash gift that would compensate the family which was giving away its daughter for her lost labor for a few years. Many ancient cultures used gift exchanges around weddings to help even out the economic changes of marriage and establish good will between the two families.

Next, levirate marriage was a way for a family to be preserved in case of disaster, when the father of the family died prematurely. A woman's brother-in-law would be required to marry her and provide an heir for his brother so that the line would not be broken—a kind of ancient life insurance. The heir would be able to support his mother eventually and continue the family. Without an heir, the family's story ends.

The "trial of the adulteress" in Leviticus 5 seems to apply only to women, even though it is in a context where some laws apply to both "male and female" (v. 3). The elaborate ritual to determine a suspected adulteress's guilt is unusual, but it is meant to establish whether or not she is ritually clean. Under the old law, adultery defiles and therefore the law requires that an adulterer be sent out of the camp to avoid contaminating others with impurity. There is no parallel trial ritual for wives accusing their husbands, but perhaps what is at stake in the ritual is the husband's honor. If he is overcome by a "spirit of jealousy" and forces his innocent wife to undergo this ritual, she will be vindicated while he will be shamed for being so ridiculously and incorrectly possessive.

Women were considered "unclean" after childbirth—seven days for boys and fourteen days for girls—because of the continuous bleeding they experience (Lv 12:1-8). Sometimes newborn girls also undergo vaginal bleeding, so the length of purification time is doubled for baby girls since there are two origins of impurity: the mother and the infant. This rule has little to do with gender inequality and more to do with the ritual purity system as a whole. Indeed, other ritual purity rules apply only to men's anatomy (Lv 15:1-18).

Additional inequalities appear in Abraham's bizarre games of wife swap with foreign rulers (Gn 12:10-20; 20:1-18) and in the wife-stealing episode in the Book of Judges (Chapter 21). But these stories often appear without comment from the narrator. No one is to assume that Abraham did the right thing in pawning off his wife. In fact, Abimelech considers it a treachery (Gn 20:9). The Judges story that finds Israelites murdering people to get virgin wife candidates and stealing women dancers at a festival is not an endorsement of these actions, but a condemnation. It is immediately followed by the sour concluding note: "In those days there was no king in Israel; every man did what was right in his own eyes" (Jgs 21:25). Not only are the stories peculiar, but the story-telling conventions are foreign to us. In order to interpret well, we need to sense these subtle clues that the text offers to us.

Third, women are often used in metaphorical contexts in the Bible to make a theological point. Some of these metaphorical scenes can be very disturbing, such as the depiction of Oholah and Oholibah in Ezekiel 23. These fictitious women represent Israel and Judah and all of their adulterous idolatry against the Lord. The prophet uses them as poetic images to describe the horror of idolatry and the severity of God's judgment against his wayward people. Other metaphorical women appear in the Bible, such as Lady Wisdom, Lady Folly, the ideal wife of Proverbs 31, and the Whore of Babylon in Revelation. These women are fictional symbols used to describe theological realities. The literary impact of the writings in which they appear depends on the power of these metaphors. When we discuss the biblical portrait of women, it is crucial that we distinguish between history and metaphor.

> *These apostolic teachings are sometimes vilified, ignored, or relegated to non-inspired status, but if the Bible is God's word, then we should at least try to understand them as they are.*

Fourth, the New Testament presents its own challenging texts on women:

> The women should keep silence in the churches. For they are not permitted to speak, but should be subordinate, as even the law says. If there is anything they desire to know, let them ask their husbands at home. For it is shameful for a woman to speak in church. (1 Cor 14:34-35)

> Let a woman learn in silence with all submissiveness. I permit no woman to teach or to have authority over men; she is to keep silent. For Adam was formed first, then Eve; and Adam was not deceived, but the woman was deceived and became a transgressor. Yet woman

> will be saved through bearing children, if she contin-
> ues in faith and love and holiness, with modesty (1 Tm
> 2:11-15).

> Wives, be subject to your husbands, as to the Lord. (Eph
> 5:22)

These apostolic teachings are sometimes vilified, ignored, or relegated to non-inspired status, but if the Bible is
God's word, then we should at least try to understand them as
they are. They head in two directions: one teaching is about the
teaching-authority structure of the Christian community; the
other is about the operation of Christian households. On the
first teaching, in 1 Corinthians 14:34, St. Paul emphasizes that
women must be silent during worship services where prophets
are speaking. But since we find women prophets elsewhere in
the New Testament (Acts 21:9; 1 Cor 11:5), he is likely referring
to conversational speaking rather than prophetic participation
in the service—that is, it would be "shameful" to interrupt and
distract from the divine service with questions and conversations. 1 Timothy 2:11-15 repeats and expands the teaching with
a reference to Adam and Eve. Here he establishes firmly that
the official teaching of the Church be conducted only by men.
As the role of the Twelve Apostles, the first bishops, the presby-
ters, and the deacons is restricted to men, Paul recognizes their
unique role in being the official stewards of the message of Jesus.
Only ordained men possess the official-teaching responsibilities
in the Church. As for beings "saved through bearing children,"
Paul cannot mean that women must have children to be saved,
especially since he praises virginity as a preferable state for a
Christian woman (1 Cor 7:25-35). Rather, he is referring to the
usual vocation of motherhood, which most Christian women
embrace as their form of "working out" one's salvation (Phil
2:12).

On the second topic, St. Paul and St. Peter express that wives should "be subject" to their husbands (see Eph 5:22, 24; Col 3:18; 1 Pt 3:1). These texts come in the context of household codes, where the apostle teaches about each role in the household. Husbands receive instruction to love their wives (Eph 5:25, 28; Col 3:19) and "live considerately" with them (1 Pt 3:7). While some want to see here an unequal power relation being established within marriage, the New Testament is pointing to a deeper reality: women desire to be loved, and men desire to be respected. When husband and wife, as equal partners, offer themselves to one another in the mode that the other can receive, a wonderful harmony in the marriage relationship emerges. The apostles recognize both the equality of and the differences between the sexes.

Finally, we can see that though the Bible emerges from a patriarchal culture, it places legal limits on the power of men as individuals and paves a way for the recognition of women's equality. The details of the old law show a respect for women and an appreciation of their important role. The Bible is not silent on the lives of women in ancient times, but actually exalts many women as heroines, such as Deborah, Esther, Jael, and Ruth. In the New Testament we find that some of Jesus' closest followers are women (Mk 15:40). In fact, the ones who stay faithful at the Crucifixion are mostly women—the male apostles, save one, fled! A woman, Mary Magdalene, is the first witness of the Resurrection (Jn 20:11-18), the "apostle to the apostles," as the early Church Fathers called her. Women are included among the significant members and benefactors of the early Church (Priscilla, Phoebe, Lydia). Indeed, the New Testament joyfully announces the equality of men and women in Christ (Gal 3:28). And ,of course, the only person chosen to be preserved from original sin and to receive the Christ Child into her own body was a woman: the Virgin Mary, Mother of God and Mother of the Church. While the Bible's stories are certainly colored by their cultural context, the Bible upholds and supports the dignity of women as created in the image and likeness of God.

Other Evils

The Bible's narrative confronts us with many inexplicable tales. A left-handed spy assassinates a fat man in his bathroom (Jgs 3:21-22). A concubine is gang-raped, then mutilated (Jgs 19:25-30). A woman kills a general with a tent peg through his head (Jgs 4:21). A prophet walks around naked for three years (Is 20:2-3). Some predict people eating their own excrement (2 Kgs 18:27) or, worse, their children (Lam 4:10; Jer 19:9). God sends a "lying spirit" into the mouths of the prophets (1 Kgs 22:22). Dogs lick up the blood of a dead king (1 Kgs 22:38). An evil queen is thrown down from a tower and trampled (2 Kgs 9:33). God even commands his prophet to bake bread over a fire of human dung (Ez 4:12). Each bizarre episode deserves its own treatment, its own book, but the parameters for interpretation are clear. We cannot reject the text of Scripture but must seek the meaning of each event or saying in the context, the history, the theology, the unity of the whole. In fact, the Old Testament especially uses many strange scenes and shocking ways of speaking to jolt its hearers out of their chairs and get them to *do something* about God's covenant with his people. The point is that God wants his people to hear him so they can respond to his loving call and avoid his fierce judgment. When evil reigns in our hearts, we cannot hear him, and sometimes we need a thunderbolt to wake us from our deaf slumber.

In the biblical cases of slavery, the treatment of women, and other difficult matters we can see how God gradually reveals himself and his ways, little by little. When we confront these texts without serious preparation, they can throw us off. We can allow their strangeness or difficulty to annoy us, or we can pass over them in blissful ignorance. But the difficult texts or the weird texts in the Bible can reveal something to us if only we are willing to dig a little deeper. If we read in context, watching carefully for clues to the divine intention at stake, we will be rewarded with a deeper level of understanding of his revelation to us. Also, it is good for us to keep in mind that there are always at least two contexts to each passage: human and divine. The human context is the culture out of which the biblical text arises, while the divine context is God's self-revelation in and through a human culture. Our job as readers is to constantly dig for the divine and look out for the literary so we can come to appreciate the power and the meaning of God's word to us.

Chapter 15

Hell: Is Permanent Punishment Just?

If there is one confounding difficulty or darkness in Scripture that is darker and more difficult than all the others, it is hell. Hell, the place of eternal punishment and unquenchable fire, the place of separation from God and permanent torture, sounds so incomprehensibly awful that we often can deal with it only by joking about it. Gary Larson's *Far Side* cartoons often parodied hell as a place where the coffee is cold and the devil welcoms people with his wry antics. We jest about things that we can't easily talk about directly. But often hell provokes not jokes but finger-pointing. If one wanted to accuse God of being unfair for choosing one ancient people among many, for instituting strange and problematic laws, for commanding *herem*-style warfare, hell tops the list of accusations against him. It seems so disproportionate to punish someone forever in fire for committing one sin. How could a just God condemn someone permanently for engaging in one very temporary act? How can we make sense of the eternal punishment of hell?

The Biblical Portrait of Hell

The biblical idea of hell takes some time to develop. In the Old Testament, we hear a lot about Sheol, or "the pit" (Ps 30:3), the place where all the dead go. Sheol was an underworld kind of place—akin to the Greek Hades, the realm of the dead—but not a place of reward or punishment. Later ideas of the afterlife usually include different destinations for the righteous and the wicked, but in the Old Testament, both the just and unjust go to Sheol. Arriving there is only a judgment if you go down to Sheol while still alive (Nm 16:30; Ps 55:15; Prv 1:12). It is a place of shadowy existence, the grave, the inevitable destiny of every person.

How could a just God condemn someone permanently for engaging in one very temporary act? How can we make sense of the eternal punishment of hell?

Yet, later in the Old Testament tradition, a notion of lasting punishment begins to develop. Isaiah mentions "devouring fire" and "everlasting burnings" as penalties for sinners (Is 33:14). In addition, we find the idea of divine recompense in the afterlife (Wis 4:18-20; Jdt 16:17). While divine retribution was expected in this life, the biblical writers indicate that often people do not receive their just deserts before death. Ecclesiastes says it best: "There is a righteous man who perishes in his righteousness, and there is a wicked man who prolongs his life in his evil-doing" (Eccl 7:15). The trouble is that life is unfair. Sometimes deserving, honorable, hardworking people suffer injustices (like Job) and the wicked prosper (Jer 12:1). The upside-downness of life, its very unfairness, indicates the need for a final righting of wrongs, a final judgment, where the poor widow will be vindicated and the oppressor will be pulled down from his throne (Lk 1:52; 18:5).

Jesus himself fills out the biblical picture of hell during his ministry. He takes up the two ways of Old Testament Wisdom literature, the path of the wise and the path of the fool, and summarizes the two possible routes to the afterlife for humanity:

Enter by the narrow gate; for the gate is wide and the way is easy, that leads to destruction, and those who enter by it are many. For the gate is narrow and the way is hard, that leads to life, and those who find it are few. (Mt 7:13-14)

In addition to the metaphor of the two paths, Jesus employs the biblical concept of final judgment, a certain day on which God will separate the sheep and the goats—a development of Ezekiel's image of God judging "between the fat sheep and the lean sheep" (Ez 34:20). In Jesus' telling, the sheep are those who cared for the hungry, the thirsty, the stranger, the naked, the prisoner, while the goats did not. The final verdict pronounced by the divine judge indicates an important aspect of hell:

> Then he will answer them, "Truly, I say to you, as you did it not to one of the least of these, you did it not to me." And they will go away into eternal punishment, but the righteous into eternal life. (Mt 25:45-46)

Notably, Jesus uses the same word, *aionion*, to indicate the duration of both heaven and hell. Both destinations are everlasting. The horror of hell is described by Jesus as the "outer darkness; there men will weep and gnash their teeth" (Mt 25:30) and "where their worm does not die, and the fire is not quenched" (Mk 9:48). It is not the kind of place you'd even want to visit. Hell always appears in the Bible as a place of terrifying punishment. Some people think that Satan reigns as king in hell, but Jesus says that there is an "eternal fire prepared for the devil and his angels" (Mt 25:41). That means Satan himself is being punished in hell. He does not reign there but suffers there. St. Paul mentions the fire that inflicts "vengeance upon those who do not know God and upon those who do not obey the gospel of our Lord Jesus" (2 Thes 1:8). That brings us back to a constant theme in discussing the dark passages: the just judgment of God.

Catholic Teaching on Hell

Hell is not a stand-alone reality, but a necessary component of God's justice. If God were to set up a system of salvation without a place of punishment, the system would be radically unjust. Thus hell is not only an expression of God's justice, but also of his love. The poet Dante famously details in his *Inferno* the words of the sign posted over the entrance to hell, which reads, "Abandon hope, all ye who enter here!" Yet few readers remember one of the lines which indicates that hell originated not only from God's justice, but from his *primo amore*, his "primal love."[63] To require immortal souls who have firmly rejected God to enter into his presence would be unloving, akin to a forced conversion or a shotgun wedding. Instead, God creates a space in the universe where these souls can live out their will to be separated from him forever. The souls in hell suffer the pain of loss (*poena damni*) since they lose the opportunity to behold God forever in the beatific vision of heaven, the ultimate fulfillment of redeemed human life. In addition, they suffer active punishments, the pain of sense (*poena sensus*), which the Bible repeatedly describes as fire. Theologians have argued over whether the fire is physical or metaphorical, but it is certainly painful. In addition to the fire, they suffer from the "worm of conscience," meaning they feel a constant remorse over their actions which led them to this place of separation and punishment.

> *If God were to set up a system of salvation without a place of punishment, the system would be radically unjust. Thus hell is not only an expression of God's justice, but also of his love.*

The important thing about hell is that no one ends up there by accident, but only "by our own free choice."[64] The book of Wisdom says of the unrighteous, "Their lawless deeds will convict them to their face" (Wis 4:20). Sin distorts our souls, and if we deliberately choose to reject God and embrace sin instead, we wind up twisting ourselves out of proper shape. The choices we make continually shape who we become, and death brings an end to the opportunity for change. Pope Benedict XVI explains the finality of our choosing:

> With death, our life-choice becomes definitive—our life stands before the judge. Our choice, which in the course of an entire life takes on a certain shape, can have a variety of forms. There can be people who have totally destroyed their desire for truth and readiness to love, people for whom everything has become a lie, people who have lived for hatred and have suppressed all love within themselves. This is a terrifying thought, but alarming profiles of this type can be seen in certain figures of our own history. In such people all would be beyond remedy and the destruction of good would be irrevocable: this is what we mean by the word hell.[65]

These persons, who have distorted their souls to such an extent that they are beyond remedy, have chosen against God, against love. While the souls of the just will live in love with God and one another for all eternity, the souls in hell have rejected love. They live in a kind of permanent isolation, where their only interaction would be with other damned souls and would only increase their misery. Love of God, love of others, the only path out of ourselves into communion, is forsaken, and the heart shaped by sin turns ever inward. The self-chosen isolation of rejecting love, of turning away from going out of ourselves, becomes permanent in hell.

Theological Issues

Now, because it is beyond the grave, exactly how God's judgment works is always a matter for reflection and even controversy.

Catholic theologians have wrestled with the necessity of baptism and the problem of what happens to babies who die without baptism, souls who have original sin, but no grave personal sin.[66] Theologians will probably continue to wrestle with these ideas and problems for some time, but in regard to unbaptized children, the Church invites us to "entrust them to the mercy of God."[67] This puts into perspective how much we can actually know about what will happen and directs our gaze back at God, to trust in his justice and mercy. He will know what to do.

Dismissing Hell

Of course, hell is not the only destination for the dead, just the most concerning! If heaven is the carrot, then hell is the stick. Unfortunately, the mystery of hell, the reality of hell, the horror and the justice of hell, are easily dismissed. Some people dismiss God because of hell, and some people dismiss hell because of God—that is, some reject God because they can't see how hell could be a just manifestation of a good God. Others, for theological reasons, can't reconcile what they know about the loving, merciful, inviting God of the Bible with a God of wrath who would punish anyone eternally. It would seem that a God who punishes people forever in hell is unjust or that his intentions fail, that he doesn't really save the world, and, ultimately, he loses—that is, the Creator of the universe is unsuccessful. Or perhaps it indicates that God is vindictive, angry, needing to inflict punishment on powerless beings to show his own power. These questions have prompted some to argue that hell is empty or that it consists in the annihilation, rather than punishment, of the soul, or that it is in some way temporary and will be eventually dissolved.

The trouble is, we can't dismiss Jesus' teachings on hell without dismissing his other teachings, so how can all the pieces of revelation come together to really show who God is and keep his love and justice together?

A few observations might help clarify how we can be people of hope and yet still believe in hell, how we can embrace mercy and punishment simultaneously. We can't know how many people are in hell, but Scripture does tell us that "a great multitude which no man could number" are in heaven (Rv 7:9). We also know that the word of the Lord does not "return empty" (Is 55:11); his intentions come to fulfillment. If God wants to save the world, as is clear in Scripture, then he will succeed. He wants everyone to come to heaven, but only by their free choice. He does not program us like robots to do his will; he invites us to choose him in love. If we are troubled, imperfect, sinful, and yet moving toward him in some way, he can purify us, change us, prepare us through the fire of purgatory. Purgatory is not hell, but a temporary place of punishment and purification, which allows imperfect souls to be cleansed and transformed by God before they enter heaven. In fact, believing in purgatory helps make believing in hell more sensible, since it shows how the mercy of God can take those who love him imperfectly and prepare them for his presence, while also providing a final destination for those who have ultimately rejected him.

> *The self-chosen isolation of rejecting love, of turning away from going out of ourselves, becomes permanent in hell.*

But how could the punishing of sinful souls forever give glory to God? How could that be an expression of God's victory? Well, remember that we end up in hell only by our own choosing. No one shoehorns us into rejecting God. It has to be a personal decision. The soul that has decided firmly to deny God and his ways does not want to live in communion with him forever. While hell might seem unfair or disproportionate to us, the Church has taught for a long time that the punishments of hell are precisely proportionate.[68] No one will suffer more or less punishment than he or she deserves. I don't think the souls in hell will be filled with anger over the injustice of their punishments but will be satisfied that they are receiving what they deserve. It might seem that the happiness of the saints in heaven would be forever marred by their knowledge of the punishment of the souls in hell, but they too will be satisfied, not because they are punitive meanies, but because the punishments show the justice of God in action.[69] The saints don't enjoy watching people being punished, but they enjoy the order of God's justice and mercy and so the execution of God's justice contributes to their joy in him.

How could the punishing of sinful souls forever give glory to God? How could that be an expression of God's victory? Well, remember that we end up in hell only by our own choosing.

While it might seem incomprehensible or at least challenging, the punishment of hell actually serves to glorify God, to reveal his nature as the just ruler of the universe. It is a harsh and radical possibility of the human will for one to reject his own Creator, his own Maker, and thus to reject his own nature as a creature. God desires to be one with us, to love us and be loved by us, to invite us into his presence for all eternity, even to free us from our sinful inclinations. But we must choose him. If we reject him, then he respects our decision and allows us to be separated from him. However, he continually holds out his hand, inviting us to the eternal banqueting table. I hope that everybody pulls up a chair.

Part III

Is There a Solution?

Part III

Is There a Solution?

Chapter 16

The Imperfections of the Old Testament

One of my students came up to me and asked: "If God so generously offers us salvation as a free gift of grace, then why does he punish sin so ruthlessly in the Old Testament? Why does he kill Nadab and Abihu with fire? Why does he try to kill Moses when he fails to circumcise his son?" The answer is not simple, as we have seen, but brings together multiple moving targets: the progressive revelation of who God is, the literary limitations of the biblical authors, and the theology of God's justice. It is tempting, at least at first, to dismiss the Old Testament, like the ancient Marcionites, but that dismissal leads to many other problems, such as trying to explain away the New Testament's frequent quoting of the Old and Jesus' role in fulfilling the Old Covenant. The way to address the question is to first make a concession and then offer an explanation. The concession is this: The Old Testament is not perfect. If it were perfect it would not need to be fulfilled. Yet Jesus talks about fulfilling the Old Testament. The New Testament continually points to how he does it, and the Church enshrines the concept of fulfillment in the Creed itself. A perfect package does not need fulfillment, but the Old Testament does.

The Imperfect Points to the Perfect

It seems odd that a perfect God would offer an imperfect revelation. Yet the very imperfection of the Old Testament revelation serves his purposes. Its status as good, yet not perfect, shows that it is still lacking in an essential way and points to the need for fulfillment, for fullness. St. Paul tells us that the Old Testament law is "holy, and the commandment is holy, just, and good" (Rom 7:12). The *Catechism* reaffirms that "the Old Testament is an indispensable part of Sacred Scripture."[70] The enduring revelatory significance of the Old Testament sounds great in the abstract, but when it gets down to the details of difficulties, it can be hard to apply. Here, St. Thomas Aquinas can help us when he teaches, "The Old Law was good indeed, but imperfect."[71] To back up his point, he cites Hebrews 7:19: "The law made nothing perfect." If the law did not have the power to make things perfect, then how could it be perfect in itself? What we have on our hands in the Old Testament is imperfection, yet revelation. Perhaps it would be better to say we have divine revelation *despite* the imperfections.

It seems odd that a perfect God would offer an imperfect revelation. Yet the very imperfection of the Old Testament revelation serves his purposes.

The Second Vatican Council teaches that the Old Testament books contain things that are "imperfect and provisional [*imperfecta et temporaria*]."[72] Certain things in the Old Testament, such as the priesthood, kingship, and tribal structure, show their temporariness readily. Once the fulfillment comes in Christ, these older institutions pass away. But the most difficult problems of the Old Testament reveal its imperfect character. Sometimes the Old Testament writers themselves could be confused about how God reveals himself, and so they explain occurrences in a way that satisfies their limited understanding, but does not *perfectly* show what is happening. They write about what is "apparent to the senses"[73] and relay events "in the way men could understand and were accustomed to."[74] For example, when the text insists that God killed David's child because of his father's sins (2 Sm 12:15) or sent a spirit to prompt prophets to actually lie (1 Kgs 22:22), we can take this imperfection into account. While I have attempted to show how such instances could line up with our conception of God's justice, we must also take into account the literary artistry of our authors. They may view all unexplainable occurrences as originating in God—that all events can be traced back to their origin in divine providence.

While in an ultimate sense this must be true, since God is the Creator of all things, oftentimes the Old Testament writers simplify the indirectness of such divine agency to a direct agency—that is, we can explain that God creates a world in which natural disasters sometimes occur: limbs fall from trees, tornadoes sweep up houses, rivers flood. These natural "evils" are part of the world which God created, so they find their origin in his will, but only indirectly since God never directly wills evil. In the same way, evils attributable to human beings who possess free will can be traced back in some way to the origin of human existence, the Creator himself, but only indirectly. Yet the Old Testament authors do not always indulge in this kind of nuance. In fact, we find God sending Satan himself to torment Job (Jb 1:12) and sending plagues upon his people after "tempting" David to sin (2 Sm 24:1), a temptation that is later attributed to Satan (1 Chr 21:1). This kind of imperfection is an incomplete, limited, inadequate explanation of a complex theological idea. The narratives of the Old Testament frequently have recourse to simplistic accounts, which don't do justice to the complexity of God's interaction with human beings.

Pope Pius XI acknowledges this difficulty when he teaches, "As should be expected in historical and didactic books, they [the Old Testament books] reflect in many particulars the imperfection, the weakness and sinfulness of man."[75] While we clearly see the weakness of the human characters in the Old Testament, it is important for us to notice the imperfection of the text itself as handed down to us.

The text of the Old Testament, while it is holy, indispensable, and irrevocable, contains problems. Those problems require careful sorting and explaining, and not "a naively literalist interpretation...which excludes every effort at understanding the Bible that takes account of its historical origins and development."[76] However, the complications of the Old Testament should not send us heading for the hills or running to a supposed "safe haven" in the New Testament alone but should drive us to seek for a deeper understanding. Pope Pius XI himself, after mentioning the difficulties, comments on how they occur "side by side with innumerable touches of greatness and nobleness," and that "nothing but ignorance and pride could blind one to the treasures hoarded in the Old Testament."[77] Digging through the difficulties of the Old Testament is a rewarding experience, a treasure hunt which allows us to unpack the hidden gems within.

> *While we clearly see the weakness of the human characters in the Old Testament, it is important for us to notice the imperfection of the text itself as handed down to us.*

The Criterion of Love

One of those gems is about getting our priorities straight. The Bible in general is not just a collection of books, histories, poems, and teachings, but it is aimed at a goal: love. The heart of the Old Testament law is love. In fact, Jesus himself quotes the Old Testament to point to the two commandments which trump all the others:

> "You shall love the Lord your God with all your heart, and with all your soul, and with all your mind. This is the great and first commandment. And a second is like it, You shall love your neighbor as yourself." (Mt 22:37-39)

We cannot divorce love from our reading of Scripture. It is where we begin and where we must end. Love of God prompts us to read his word, and love must carry us through to the end of the process of interpretation. St. Augustine insists on the priority of love when reading and explaining the Bible:

> Whoever, then, thinks that he understands the Holy Scriptures, or any part of them, but puts such an interpretation upon them as does not tend to build up this twofold love of God and our neighbour, does not yet understand them as he ought.[78]

For Augustine, all of Scripture leads us back to love. Any interpretation which contradicts love, destroys love, or discourages love, cannot be a true one. All of our reading of Scripture must come together in a beautiful whole, which holds in balance Old and New Testament, hard and easy passages, the parts we like and the parts we don't. But the challenge of arriving at a correct interpretation of Scripture cannot be let go in the name of ease. Scripture is meant to challenge us. Nor can we introduce contradictions into God as if he were an erratic persona, sometimes wrathful and sometimes huggable. The justice and mercy of God, his righteousness and his love, his fierceness and his clemency, must be honored, held in tension, and appreciated in their fullness. Ultimately, however, all paths of interpretation must lead back to one route: love. And as Augustine emphasizes, this love has two dimensions: love of God and love of neighbor. Reading Scripture should fan the flame of love in our hearts and drive us on to adopt a spiritual life of loving service, to imitate Jesus, the king who washes our feet.

Fulfillment

While imperfection might seem bothersome, it actually gives us a thirst for perfection. Incompleteness makes us long for completeness. Even in the Old Testament itself, there is continued expression of longing for fulfillment. Ecclesiastes points out the seemingly pointless drudgery of life. The prophets anticipate a coming messiah figure who would redeem Israel. The exiled Jews long to return to the Promised Land yet never come into full possession of it. The Old Testament does not satisfy the longing that it prompts. Instead, it constantly increases it, pouring fuel on the fire of hunger for justice, for God, for righteousness and vindication. God waits until the right moment, until the "fullness of time" (Gal 4:4), to send his Son who will embody the complete revelation of the Father. Jesus sees his own role, not as destroying an old religion or inventing a new one, but as fulfilling the Old Testament: "Think not that I have come to abolish the law and the prophets; I have come not to abolish them but to fulfill them" (Mt 5:17). Jesus fulfills the promises and hopes of the Old Testament. The tragic covenant-breaking of the people of the Old Testament will be undone, and the promises which God granted to Abraham back at the beginning of the story will reach their final stage of fulfillment. Through Jesus, God will bless "all the families of the earth" (Gn 12:3), as he had promised to Abraham. Rather than having only an exclusive relationship with one people, God will break open the doors to salvation for all nations and invite everyone to share in the blessings of Abraham, the father of faith.

> *Reading Scripture should fan the flame of love in our hearts and drive us on to adopt a spiritual life of loving service, to imitate Jesus, the king who washes our feet.*

The problematic, partial, incomplete revelation of the Old Testament will give way to the perfect revelation of the Father in his Son, Jesus. The blessings, which had been restricted to one people, and had been repeatedly spurned through disobedience, will now expand to everyone who has faith in Jesus. The old law, with all of its limitations, served its purpose: to reveal the holiness of God and the sinfulness of man, to show how incredibly sinful sin really is, in order that we might come to repentance and faith. Many of the terrifying judgments we witness in the Old Testament—whether of Nadab and Abihu or others—serve God's pedagogical purpose: to teach us about who we are and about who he is. They show us how sinful and desperately in need of his mercy we are and how he is holy and able to save. Although we explained the concept of the divine pedagogy at the beginning of this book, we will return to reflect on what we have learned about it from delving into the details of devilishly problematic passages.

Chapter 17

Students of God the Teacher

Reading the Bible is much like visiting a foreign country. The people speak differently. The terrain is new to us. The food tastes alien. The customs, habits, laws, rituals, and ways of life are remote from our experience. While we have obvious human similarities to everyone we encounter—the need to sleep, work, eat, and so on—it is hard for us to quickly adjust to our new surroundings. I think this is why our reading of the Old Testament can be so jarring. We are often presented with a sanitized picture of it. The verses people quote are the "nice" ones. The Lectionary itself excises difficult texts from the readings for liturgy. The difficulties are often just glossed over, forgotten, or hidden in a closet of skeletons. Then, when we actually encounter the text for ourselves, as it stands, without deletions, trouble can arise. We had expected a nice, comforting religious book, full of encouragement and hope, but while we find some of that, we also find judgment, punishment, polygamy, and wars wrapped in a complex web of ancient customs that we do not readily grasp. The bizarreness of it all can be off-putting. It is tempting to put the book down rather than wrestle with it to extract its significance.

However, to set it down would run afoul of the New Testament's advice. St. Paul insists that "*all* scripture is inspired by God and profitable for teaching, for reproof, for correction, and for training in righteousness" (1 Tm 3:16, emphasis added). For St. Paul the word *scripture* did not yet include the New Testament, since much of it had not yet been written. He's talking about the Old Testament! Notice that the first value he mentions is "teaching." The Old Testament teaches us about the nature of God, who he is, what he does, and how he saves. The *Catechism* teaches, "The books of the Old Testament bear witness to the whole divine pedagogy of God's saving love: these writings 'are a storehouse of sublime teaching on God and of sound wisdom on human life, as well as a wonderful treasury of prayers; in them, too, the mystery of our salvation is present in a hidden way.' "[79]

What is the divine pedagogy? It is God's way of teaching us. He teaches us according to our nature—that is, in a way that we can understand, a way that is suited to the way we are built. He teaches us in stages, gradually revealing himself and his plan. He teaches us in a way that conveys his grace, his help not only to understand what he reveals but to live it out. St. John Paul II teaches, "Throughout sacred history, especially in the Gospel, God himself used a pedagogy that must continue to be a model for the pedagogy of faith."[80]

God's way of teaching is the best way of teaching, and it would behoove us to follow his example when we teach. But as readers of the Old Testament, we find ourselves in the shoes of students, wishing to learn, to understand what our Teacher has to say. So when we encounter a difficult moment in salvation history and are tempted to turn away with revulsion, perhaps we should ask ourselves, "What is God trying to teach me through this text?" Answering that question will be well worth it.

Why the Old Law?

One persistent question that affects all of our Bible reading is how to deal with the Old Testament law and its story. Why would God call Abraham, found a people, grant them a land, give them a law through Moses, give them a king in David, and then eventually banish them from the land and allow their kingdom to fall to foreign powers? Why not just send Jesus right away and forgo the trials of the Old Testament? The mystery of God's pattern of revelation is not easy to unravel, but St. Paul sheds some light on why God chose this path. Paul argues, as I mentioned earlier, that the law of Moses is a *paidagogos*, a teacher, a tutor, a schoolmaster, to bring us to faith (Gal 3:24). It is not a stand-alone miracle of God's revelation, but a part of his overarching plan to bring humanity back to himself. I have heard it said that the Mosaic law was like a series of protocols that scientists follow when dealing with nuclear material. They measure radiation with Geiger counters, count their exposure with dosimetry badges, and carefully insulate radioactive materials in special containers and storage units. The danger of radiation exposure is so serious that all these carefully crafted rituals protect the personnel from harm. In a similar way, the Old Testament law provided a set of practices and rituals for sin and ritual impurity to avoid contaminating that which was holy. Since Jesus had not yet come, there was no way to truly get rid of the guilt of sin (Heb 10:4), so it could only be confined, restricted, and cautiously contained.

> *When we encounter a difficult moment in salvation history and are tempted to turn away with revulsion, perhaps we should ask ourselves, "What is God trying to teach me through this text?"*

The old law teaches us about the gravity of sin. St. Paul says that commandments came in order that sin "might become sinful beyond measure" (Rom 7:13). Without a law "sin lies dead" (Rom 7:8) in that it is undefined, unregulated, evil, but not fully shown to be what it is. The ancient pagans worshiped false gods but did not possess the Ten Commandments to show them the exact violation of the divine order they were committing. But the Mosaic law comes like a magnifying glass or microscope to show precisely how sinful sin really is. The law is like a highlighter that displays the true evil of sinful behavior, of violating the way God made us and rejecting his plan for our lives. In fact, the Church teaches that death is a result of sin: "Death was therefore contrary to the plans of God the Creator and entered the world as a consequence of sin."[81] The Old Testament reveals the truly deadly consequences of sin. The law in itself is "holy and just and good" (Rom 7:12), but it does not save us. The law is like a mirror that shows us how dirty we are, but we can't wash ourselves clean with a mirror. Only with the water of redemption, the free gift of grace which is obtained through faith and baptism, can we be cleansed.

The Old Testament, through its stories, practices, laws, and prayers, prepares us for the final stage of revelation in the life and ministry of Jesus.

Thus the purpose of the Old Testament law was not to save but to teach. By "typology" Old Testament characters and themes foreshadow Christ and his coming. Adam, Moses, David, and other biblical characters are "types" of Christ. Jesus is like Adam, but instead of bringing death through sin, he brings life through righteousness (Rom 5:12-21). Jesus is like Moses in that he gives us a new law, the law of love (Jn 13:34). Jesus is like David, a righteous king reigning forever over God's people (Mt 21:9; Rv 22:16).

Even the rituals of Old Testament worship prepare for the sacraments of the New Covenant. Circumcision foreshadows baptism. The sacrifices of the Temple prepare for the ultimate sacrifice of Christ. The Passover meal reaches fulfillment in the Last Supper. The Old Testament, through its stories, practices, laws, and prayers, prepares us for the final stage of revelation in the life and ministry of Jesus.

Looking Back at the Lessons

As we have looked at some of the messy parts of the biblical picture, it might be worth summarizing how these stories can teach us about God. The killing in the Old Testament acknowledges that the plan has gone wrong, that death has entered the story through sin. It also shows us that sin orients us toward death and that it brings death upon us. God reveals the lethal orientation of sin in the capital punishments included in the old law and in various stories where he responds to human sin with the punishment of death. We have seen that God always rejects child sacrifice, and condemns those who practice it. However, sometimes children do become victims of death on account of their parents' sins. But even then, death is not the end of the story, and we can hold out hope for these children that God's mercy will ultimately rescue them. God shows from the beginning a "purpose of election" in that he chooses Abraham, Isaac, Jacob, and their descendants to receive his promises, his law, his covenant, his revelation. Though he chooses to reveal himself to a certain people, he opens the plan of salvation to everyone at the coming of Christ. Our sufferings and the sufferings of the innocent find a redemptive meaning in Christ and are not meaningless experiences, but are ones that can lead us by grace deeper into the mystery of God's love. The strange practices in the Bible, whether polygamy, slavery, or other behaviors, are included in the story, not as guides for how to live, but as the opposite. The problems with polygamy illumine God's plan of monogamy. The Old Testament law reveals human dignity by how it restricts the practice of slavery. Finally, hell exists as a radical possibility of the human will, a place for those who ultimately reject God. Yet God provides an avenue for repentance in this life and purification in the next (in purgatory), with the hope that everyone will turn to him and receive his free gift of salvation. The difficult, dark passages in the Bible might never be our favorite ones, but they can and do teach about who God is, what he does, and how he saves those who reach out to him.

Spiritual Interpretation

Christians have long struggled with how to read the dark passage in a way that is spiritually beneficial, that is in accord with St. Augustine's "charity principle." After we get through the difficult work of coming to grips with the literal sense and the majesty of God's just judgment, how do we pray with texts that talk of killing the Canaanites or smashing Babylonian babies? Rather than just excluding these texts from our prayer life, Christian tradition provides an avenue of spiritual interpretation that helps us modify our incorporation of these texts into our spiritual vocabulary. The "Canaanites" that we see the ancient Israelites commanded to conquer become the inner "Canaanites" of temptation and sin. Our calling is not to go defeat people in battle, but to defeat the sinful inclinations in our own hearts through relying on God's grace and embracing his discipline. Smashing the little ones of Babylon (Ps 137:6) is transformed into uprooting the first sproutings of sin in our hearts, not allowing the "spiritual Babylon" within to regrow. In addition, the "enemies" of the Psalms are not human beings who are out to get us, but demonic powers who seek to tempt and harm us: "For we are not contending against flesh and blood, but against the principalities, against the powers, against the world rulers of this present darkness, against the spiritual hosts of wickedness in the heavenly places" (Eph 6:12). While it is important not to jump over the hard work of understanding the literal sense,[82] in the end we must arrive at a place where we can cohesively appropriate the message of Scripture and allow ourselves to be conformed to God through our reading of his word. Spiritual interpretation helps us engage with the word and to reengage certain texts that we might have stopped reading because of their challenges.

The *Catechism* outlines the senses of Scripture in two major categories: literal and spiritual. The literal sense covers the language, grammar, history, and literary features of the text. Aiming at the literal sense is aiming at the sense the author meant to convey. The spiritual sense can be subdivided into the allegorical sense, the moral sense, and the anagogical sense. For example, the Temple in the Bible, in the literal sense, refers to the building in Jerusalem where the ancient Jews worshiped. But allegorically, the Temple refers to Christ's body offered for us (Jn 2:21). In the moral sense, the Temple refers to our bodies, which ought to be used for moral, not immoral, purposes (1 Cor 6:19). In the anagogical sense, the Temple points forward to the heavenly sanctuary where the saints worship God for all eternity (Rv 15:5-8). Not every text or idea will fit as neatly into the four senses of Scripture, but they give us a pattern to follow when we are looking for the meaning of Scripture beyond the literal.

Spiritual interpretation helps us engage with the word and to reengage certain texts that we might have stopped reading because of their challenges.

By being attentive to what God is teaching through even the most difficult Scripture texts, we can become students of God the Teacher. He wouldn't have given us his word if he didn't intend it for our instruction. In fact, St. Benedict asks, "What page, what passage of the inspired books of the Old and New Testaments is not the truest of guides for human life?"[83] The word of God is meant to teach us, to instruct us, and to train us. A good student of it must embrace it with humility, but not with naiveté. Some of its teaching cannot be easily grasped and so must be struggled through. The process of grappling with the difficult texts, fitting each puzzle piece into the picture of how God wants us to think and live, is meant to conform us more to his likeness.

Now it is time for us to climb the highest mountain of Scripture and grapple with the most difficult and most important challenge of all: the Cross.

Chapter 18

The Cross: The Greatest (In)Justice

It is easy to forget the darkness of the Cross. In considering the dark and difficult parts of Scripture, we might overlook the darkest passage of all, where the killing of God is depicted in the most horrific way. The strangeness of the Old Testament problems such as polygamy, child sacrifice, and ancient warfare are easy to hold at arm's length as if they were curiosities from a bygone era. Yet the dark passages of Scripture reveal at their core a God who is not merely a lawgiver or ruler, but an empathetic and merciful Father, willing to send his own Son to die for the very people who broke his law. At the Cross, the dark passages of Scripture reach their apex. God reveals his mercy and his justice simultaneously in the terrifying crucifixion of his Son. In the deepest darkness, the brightest light shines.

One of the strangest things about Christianity is the Cross. Front and center in every Catholic church is a crucifix, a depiction of a man dying on a cross. Since crosses and crucifixes have been around in Western culture since ancient times, the incongruity of them often escapes us. But for an ancient Roman, our crucifix would be akin to an artistic depiction of a man being hung on a gallows or executed in an electric chair—a startling artwork meant to shake us out of our comfort zone. The Cross is a paradox, a meeting point of heaven and earth, the junction of justice and mercy, the place of punishment and redemption. A crucifix requires interpretation. If you don't know the story, you won't understand it.

The very shocking nature of the crucifixion of Jesus caused the ancients to recoil. "For the word of the cross is folly to those who are perishing, but to us who are being saved it is the power of God" (1 Cor 1:18). The "folly" of the Cross is that it looks like a loss. It looks as if God tried to save the world through a man and failed. The messenger was shot. Jesus' opponents couldn't understand what he was doing and insisted that he come down from the cross and save himself to show God's power (Mt 27:40), not realizing that it was through his voluntary act of suffering on the cross that he was actually enacting God's power to save. St. Paul refers to the Cross as a "stumbling block" (Gal 5:11). It is confounding. It looks like a failure when in fact it is a victory. The biblical presentation of the mystery of the Cross shows us that it unites two seemingly opposed attributes of God: his justice and his mercy.

The "folly" of the Cross is that it looks like a loss. It looks as if God tried to save the world through a man and failed.

The Mercy of the Cross

The basics of redemption are something we have heard many times: All have sinned and fallen short of the glory of God (Rom 3:23). The wages of sin is death (Rom 6:23), and so because of our sin we deserved death. As we explored above, death is a consequence of sin.[84] But God in his wisdom and love sent his Son Jesus to die for us and free us from sin. "For God so loved the world that he gave his only Son, that whoever believes in him should not perish but have eternal life" (Jn 3:16). God did not intend for Adam and Eve to die, but they ate the fruit of the tree and therefore were subject to death (Gn 2:17). Through their sin death entered the world (Rom 5:12).

To undo the curse of sin and free sinners from slavery to it, God decided to act.

God sent his Son Jesus to die for us even though we didn't deserve it. "God shows his love for us in that while we were yet sinners Christ died for us" (Rom 5:8). Jesus takes our sins upon himself. By his self-sacrifice, he pays the ransom; he cancels the debt of our sin, nailing our promissory note to the cross (Col 2:14). "In this is love, not that we loved God but that he loved us and sent his Son to be the expiation for our sins" (1 Jn 4:10). The Cross shows God's *love* for us, that he would give up his Son, and Jesus' love for us, that he would voluntarily undergo crucifixion. It also shows the Son's *obedience* to the Father: he "became obedient unto death, even death on a cross" (Phil 2:8). The Cross is also a *sacrifice*. Jesus is both the priest and the sacrificial victim who offers a final and universal sacrifice of himself on the altar of the Cross: "We have been sanctified through the offering of the body of Jesus Christ once for all" (Heb 10:10). Through the Cross, Jesus *redeems* us. We were held captive under the slavery of sin (Rom 6:17), but he sets us free from that bondage and servitude.

The power of his Cross will never be used up but will always be able to redeem those who believe in him.

The Plan

But how does Jesus' suffering and death actually save us? If any other person were to go die on a cross, it would not change my life, and certainly not my eternal destination.[85] Why does Jesus' death have a universal effect? Why does it undo the disobedience of Adam? This is where God's plan comes in. It would be easy to think that Pontius Pilate or the Sanhedrin or the Roman soldiers or Judas was fully responsible for Jesus' death, as if it were an accident, something that God did not intend, but something out of which he was able to bring good. But that would contradict how St. Peter himself interprets the Cross: "This Jesus, delivered up according to the definite plan and foreknowledge of God, you crucified and killed by the hands of lawless men" (Acts 2:23). God knew and planned from the beginning that Jesus would die in this way. He "died for our sins *in accordance with* the scriptures" (1 Cor 15:3, emphasis added). In fact, God "did not spare his own Son but gave him up for us all" (Rom 8:32). The Father places all the sins of the whole world on Jesus' shoulders: "For our sake he made him to be sin who knew no sin, so that in him we might become the righteousness of God" (2 Cor 5:21). The sacrifice of the Cross was part of the plan from the beginning. It was not an accident. It was not a failure. In addition, Jesus' death differed from every other death because he was God. His suffering is the most extreme suffering of all time because he had an infinite ability to experience suffering. His suffering incorporates all punishment for all sin for all people for all time. In fact, the Church holds that his suffering is superabundant, that he does not just make satisfaction for the sins of the saved, but for the whole world (1 Jn 2:2).[86] The power of his Cross will never be used up but will always be able to redeem those who believe in him.

The (In)Justice of the Cross

The greatest sin in human history was the killing of Christ. To betray and murder the innocent is wrong, but to kill God is the highest crime: *deicide*.[87] Jesus had done no wrong. He was "holy, blameless, unstained, separated from sinners, and exalted above the heavens" (Heb 7:26). If it were unjust to kill anyone—as we know it is from the Ten Commandments—then to kill Jesus would be the most radically unjust killing imaginable. So what does Jesus' radically unjust death accomplish other than showing us how much God loves us and how merciful he is? Is it more than just a display of God's affection for us? Yes.

God did not have to crucify his Son. He could have snapped his fingers and saved us by divine act.[88] He could have, but he didn't. Why? I think the answer to this mystery lies in God's justice. He could have forgiven us without requiring satisfaction, but Jesus dies on the cross as an act of satisfaction. He *atones* for our sins by his suffering. That atonement is the expiation, the ransom, the satisfaction for our sins.[89] He takes our punishment upon himself. God "sent his own Son in the likeness of sinful flesh and for sin, condemned sin in the flesh" (Rom 8:3). "For our sake he made him to be sin who knew no sin, so that in him we might become the righteousness of God" (2 Cor 5:21). Jesus becomes "sin" in order that sin might be condemned. So the Cross reveals the horror of sin, its evil, its drama, its terrible consequences, its orientation toward death. "The sting of death is sin, and the power of sin is the law" (1 Cor 15:56). But Jesus was innocent; he did not deserve to die; he is the spotless victim, so his death works differently. By taking our sin upon himself and dying, Jesus displays the just judgment of God. His Cross reveals the utter sinfulness of sin and the perfect justice of God, which requires the satisfaction for sin. It saves us by virtue of the perfect atonement it enacts. "This was to show God's righteousness, because in his divine forbearance he had passed over former sins; it was to prove at the present time that he himself is righteous and that he justifies him who has faith in Jesus" (Rom 3:25-26). Jesus' crucifixion proves that God is just in that he requires satisfaction or atonement for sin. But it also proves his ability to justly save us by making us just through faith in Jesus, the only perfect God-man capable of taking the sins of the world on his shoulders. By faith and baptism, we receive God's righteousness and share in the victory that Christ won on the cross.[90]

While through Adam's sin we all "died" because we were under the power of sin and death, now through Christ's sacrifice we are freed from the power of sin and given life everlasting. "Then as one man's trespass led to condemnation for all men, so one man's act of righteousness leads to acquittal and life for all men" (Rom 5:18). The evil contagion of sin introduced by Adam's disobedience now is confronted and overcome by the antidote, the vaccine, given in the death and resurrection of Jesus. He delivers us from the power of sin and offers us the promise of eternal life in him through his Cross.

> *The Cross embodies our worst fears: fears of suffering, death, punishment, rejection; and our greatest hopes: forgiveness, redemption, eternal life.*

The Cross is a paradox. At one and the same time it condemns the evil of sin and delivers us from its power. It displays the justice of God, who demands satisfaction for every offense against him in the suffering of Jesus: "It was the will of the LORD to bruise him" (Is 53:10). Yet it also shows the extreme mercy and love of God, who would willingly offer his Son for our sake. It demonstrates what evil humans are capable of, killing God, and yet how God is able to bring immense good out of such evil and that it was in his plan to do so from the beginning. The Cross shows the disobedience of man, while revealing the obedience of Christ. It shows us the perfect sacrificial victim offered by the perfect priest, himself. The Cross embodies our worst fears: fears of suffering, death, punishment, rejection; and our greatest hopes: forgiveness, redemption, eternal life. When we stop and take a second look at a crucifix and allow ourselves to be startled by its horror, its contradiction, its power, perhaps then the paradox will start to come together. In the Cross, somehow we can share both in Christ's sufferings and in his victory (2 Cor 1:5). It is not only a symbol of sorrow, but an emblem of triumph. The greatest injustice has become the greatest act of justice and the greatest extension of God's mercy.

The Gospel of John insists, "The light shines in the darkness and the darkness has not overcome it" (1:5). The Cross that was a symbol of death and darkness has been converted into a symbol of hope. It is no longer about death, but about the defeat of death. God has trumped death at its own game and beaten back the forces of darkness. The shocking horror of Abraham nearly knifing his son to death is brought to fever pitch, with God, in his fierce justice, allowing his own Son to be executed. He removes the sin by which we brought divine judgment on ourselves and places it on his Son. In the darkness of divine judgment, we find the light of hope, a light that cannot be snuffed out.

Chapter 19

Mysterious Incompleteness

The dark passages of Scripture present us with problems to solve. But even if we formulate explanations, clarify the obscure, and rework our thoughts, we are bound to come up short. We love airtight, compact, succinct solutions, but the world that God created, God himself, and his word are not that simple. Scripture overwhelms us with its beauty at times, but also frustrates us with its complexity. Scholars have been writing books about the Book for millennia, and by the looks of any publisher's new titles list, the writing will continue. Yet the obscurity or challenge of certain passages should not discourage us from the quest. Rather, they whet our appetite for a deeper understanding, a more complete picture. But that picture we are able to see will always be mysteriously incomplete.

Our questions remain only incompletely answered. While God gives us a good solid glimpse into who he is through Scripture and Tradition, he cannot be encompassed by the revelation he offers us. It is not as if we see him face to face, but as if we were looking through a pinhole into eternity, overwhelmed by the tiny shaft of light which we are granted. Or rather, as St. Paul puts it: "For now we see in a mirror dimly, but then face to face. Now I know in part; then I shall understand fully, even as I have been fully understood" (1 Cor 13:12). Ancient mirrors like the ones manufactured in Corinth were made of polished metal, so the reflection would be very poor compared with modern mirrors. Christian life on earth likewise has a mysterious dimness to it. We live in hope of what is to come but only partially possess it. God has given us "his Spirit in our hearts as a guarantee," a down payment on eternal life (2 Cor 1:22), but we do not yet have the complete package. Our union with him in prayer and the sacraments is always limited on earth by our humanity.

When we confront difficulties in Scripture and work our way through the challenging task of interpretation, sometimes we will still come out at the end of the process not fully satisfied.

Unfortunately, our human limitations can be frustrating. We long for the satisfaction of knowing—knowing for certain—exactly who God is, how he operates, how much he loves us. When we confront difficulties in Scripture and work our way through the challenging task of interpretation, sometimes we will still come out at the end of the process not fully satisfied. While some of the problems of the ancients we can hold at arm's length, undeserved suffering is especially troubling since it is a lived problem, not an abstract notion. Real people with real circumstances daily confront the reality of suffering. Usually they need a helping hand or a hug rather than a theological explanation. Even though we are confident that all human suffering can be a redemptive path to holiness when united with Christ's sufferings,[91] it still pains us and occasionally overwhelms us. When we feel overwhelmed by suffering, confusion, frustration, or our own inability to avoid sin, we can turn to the God of mystery, who reveals himself to us and simply respond to his simple command: "Be still and know that I am God" (Ps 46:10). Sometimes the mirror is so dark, the problem so obscure, or the suffering so intense, that silence is the only path to peace. Our hearts can tolerate only so much paradox before they need a rest.

In those moments, we need to recall our faith, our trust in the God who is ultimately trustworthy. If he could rescue Daniel from the lions and Paul from prison, if he could create the sun and raise Lazarus from the dead, then surely we can trust him. He is not a random, inconsistent god, but a God who reliably saves, blesses, and delivers. Though his judgment is fearsome, he is still the God of mercy, the good shepherd who lays his life down for the sheep, the rabbi who eats with tax collectors and sinners, the father who welcomes back his prodigal son, the one who cares for the widow and orphan. Though we cannot fully know him in this life, we can fully trust him. Though we cannot see him face to face, yet we can behold him in Word and Sacrament. Our God does not leave us stranded in a vast universe without a toehold on eternity, but shows us something of who he is through Scripture and through his Church. And when Scripture challenges us, his grace comes to aid our understanding.

Why the Difficulties?

Why does God grant us a revelation that is full of so many difficulties? St. Augustine contemplates precisely why we find so many challenging passages in Scripture. He says:

> The obscurity of the divine word has certainly this advantage, that it causes many opinions about the truth to be stated and discussed, each reader seeing some fresh meaning in it, yet, whatever is said to be meant by an obscure passage should be either confirmed by the testimony of obvious facts, or should be asserted in other and less ambiguous texts. This obscurity is beneficial, whether the sense of the author is at last reached after the discussion of many other interpretations, or whether, though that sense remain concealed, other truths are brought out by the discussion of the obscurity.[92]

For Augustine, obscurity is good! Difficult to interpret passages prompt discussion, analysis, and the struggle to grasp the meaning intended. For him, this is a good thing, something that God intended. In Augustine's view, Scripture is not a dead letter to be tucked away on dusty shelves, but a living Word which needs to be thought about, wrestled with, and actively discussed with friends. The discussion of difficult texts, obscure phrases, and "dark passages" is where the meaning gets hashed out. Augustine gives the conversation guide rails by clarifying that facts and other biblical texts should inform our discussion, showing that we should be reading the Bible as a whole and not just reading one section. In addition, our interpretation of Scripture should be bounded by the teaching of the Church and constantly directed toward love. The very process of grappling with the text is a benefit for us. If it weren't difficult, we wouldn't be as likely to discuss it, and if we didn't discuss it, we would not encounter the "other truths" which the conversation brings up. Yet even if Scripture stimulates an interesting discussion, sometimes we still walk away with a sinking feeling of dissatisfaction, with our questions yet unanswered.

Scripture is not a dead letter to be tucked away on dusty shelves, but a living Word which needs to be thought about, wrestled with, and actively discussed with friends.

The Clarity of Death

God could have offered us a mere list of dos and don'ts, but instead he offered us the multifaceted literature which constitutes the Bible. Poetry, history, theology, prophecy, biography, and apocalypse fill the pages between Genesis and Revelation. They offer us a snapshot of what God is like, how he invites us, and how we can respond to him. But even if we master every chapter and verse, our picture of him will always be a little hazy, a little unclear, a little incomplete. The dark passages of Scripture, which challenge us to think hard, often leave us with a sense of that insufficiency in our guts. They remind us that in heaven we won't be reading about God but looking at him. The only partially satisfying answers we can give to the burning questions we have will finally be answered, clarified, put into divine perspective.

The incompleteness of our understanding in this life, I think, should make us look forward to the clarity which death brings. It is not as though we should long for death, but that death will usher in an understanding that far surpasses what we know now. As St. Paul says in the passage I quoted above: "Then I shall understand fully" (1 Cor 13:12). Our culture vacillates back and forth between fear of death and fascination with it. The ancient Hebrews hoped to be buried with their ancestors, while many in our culture want their ashes sprinkled over their favorite lake. Death is important because it is the last step of our earthly pilgrimage. It should not be trivialized and cannot be ignored. Death is the separation of the soul from the body. Though it seems like an end, it is just a new beginning. "In death, God calls man to himself."[93] It invites us into a new and deeper relationship with God. While it seems to cut us off from life, it can actually be for our "gain" (Phil 1:21) and the change that brings us to resurrection life (2 Tm 2:11). Catholic spirituality refers to preparing oneself for a "good death," and in the Liturgy of the Hours we actually pray for a "peaceful death." Death is a trial, a struggle, often seen as a final spiritual battle for the soul. To have a "good death" is to persevere to the end, to make it through the last challenge of our life on earth. Through repentance, prayer, and a life of faithful service to God, we can prepare ourselves for that moment, which does not just snuff out our earthly life but actually leads us into further light. The limitations of our earthly existence will fall away as God bids us into an eternity of perfect love, where all of our longings will be fulfilled.

Our knowledge of anything and everything on earth is limited. Today we learn something new; tomorrow we forget it; next year we need to relearn it. The challenges we face in just keeping a handle on all the things we need to know is daunting enough, let alone the pursuit of topics we are just curious about! When it comes to our knowledge of God, we want to embrace its importance but humbly acknowledge how incomplete it really is. Though we long to know deeply, fully, and perfectly, our knowledge of him will always be shallow, partial, and imperfect until we see him face to face. Rather than discourage us, the incompleteness of our knowledge should cause us to rejoice in the fact that the all-knowing God has chosen to reveal himself to us. We need him.

The challenge of the dark passages of Scripture hinges on this dichotomy: We can either allow ourselves to become exasperated by them, or we can allow them to drive us on in joyful discovery of the truth.

Whether we think of divine revelation as a pinhole through which to glimpse the Divine or as a polished piece of metal in which we try to discern our reflection, the point is that on earth, our thirst for knowledge cannot be fully quenched. Indeed, we must put up with our own limitations in every area of life—we might drive cars but not know how to build them, or live in houses wired for electricity without knowing how electricity really works. In fact, the reservoir of knowledge is inexhaustible. You could study every subject imaginable, read as many books as possible throughout your whole life, and still have an eternity of new things to learn. Learning is one of the joys of life because it is so inexhaustible, but its very inexhaustibility can be exasperating. The challenge of the dark passages of Scripture hinges on this dichotomy: We can either allow ourselves to become exasperated by them, or we can allow them to drive us on in joyful discovery of the truth. Augustine suggests they should lead us to discussion of ideas and discovery of truths we had not noticed at first. Yet in all humility, we must recognize that some of the tensions we notice will not be subdued, some of the mysteries will never be fully solved, until we see God face to face. Instead we can embrace the mystery and stand in awe of an infinite God willing to love and teach broken creatures like us. "Now hope that is seen is not hope" (Rom 8:24). We do not yet see, but we hope. We do not yet fully know, but we look forward to completion. The paradox we see may persist, but the paradox of unseen hope perseveres yet more.

Chapter 20

Mercy Triumphs over Judgment

Enigmas make us think. Any tough problem demands some serious thought. That is why the founder of IBM, Thomas Watson, put up signs around the company saying, "THINK." Company-issued paper notebooks had it on their covers (The original "ThinkPad"!). Perhaps we would do well to write "Think!" on the covers of our Bibles. When we love God and approach his Word in reverence and awe, we come with our hearts in our hands, looking for God to speak to us, inspire us, breathe his life into us. But sometimes we forget to bring along our thinking cap. Knowledge and love go hand in hand, and as we have seen, God's Word demands some thinking through on our part. Opponents of the Word will often reduce the complex problems of the Bible to simplistic either-or problems, which have the appearance of erudition but often actually contain logical errors. To seriously confront the difficulties in the Bible, we must put aside wishful thinking and consider them head-on. That is exactly what we have been trying to do in this book.

Our Journey through the Dark Passages

We have seen why it is so important to address the problems: to respond to critics and to prevent crises of faith. We have also taken a look at the inadequate solutions to the problems: the "shrug," the over-spiritualization of the text, throwing out the

Old Testament, and making ourselves the moral judges of the Bible. Our gut reactions to the shocking events we find in the text indicate our moral sensitivity, but we can't stop at the reaction. We must think through the problems we confront and see how they fit into the whole picture of Scripture, Old and New Testaments. We have confronted the issue of killing in the Bible. God clearly commands us not to kill, yet sometimes in the Bible he strikes people down, or commands others to do the same according to his law. What emerges from our discussion, though, is not an easy explanation, but one that finds the origin of death in human sin and the mastery of God over life and death. We have investigated the Old Testament approach to children in the conquest of Canaan and in terms of pagan human sacrifice, showing that children are not normally the targets of violent actions on the part of God's people and that God explicitly and repeatedly rejects child sacrifice.

To seriously confront the difficulties in the Bible, we must put aside wishful thinking and consider them head-on.

In the Old Testament, God chooses a particular people for his own, not in order to exclude everyone else, but to entrust them with his revelation and prepare the way for his Son. God actually extends his salvific blessing through the Chosen People to all the families of the earth (Gn 12:3). Election opens the door to universal salvation and God wills the salvation of all people. We have also briefly reflected on the issue of innocent suffering and sought to find an answer in the mystery of iniquity and the ultimate judgment of God. Particular issues such as polygamy and slavery stand out as needing historical explanation and contextualization. We have seen how polygamy does not exemplify God's plan for marriage and is eventually quashed. Slavery is an affront to human dignity, which biblical law and teaching restricts, limits, and criticizes. Misogyny is not from God. The biblical texts that seem to denigrate women can be explained and interpreted to reveal a harmony and complementarity between the sexes in which men and women share equal dignity before God. Last, the eternal punishment of hell itself, which seems monstrously unjust to some, fits into the plan of a loving and merciful God who will not force his creatures to love him, but provides a way for them to permanently reject him if they so choose.

The judgment of God in the Old Testament is the way in which he expresses his mercy toward the oppressed.

All of the difficulties of the Bible culminate in the awesome paradox of the Cross, in which God's loving mercy and fierce justice are simultaneously put on display. Jesus' death reveals a great mystery of God's plan of salvation—that he would have mercy on us through an act of justice, where Christ the perfect Lamb of God becomes a sin offering for us. He took our sins upon himself and so atoned for them. We cannot save ourselves by our own efforts. We cannot make satisfaction to God for our sins. But Jesus makes satisfaction for us by his death and delivers salvation to us by his resurrection. We can only receive what he has to offer as a gift by faith. Righteousness before God is not a personal achievement, but a grace. The seeming defeat of the Cross gives way to the glory of the Resurrection, and we are invited to share in it. No one in heaven, except Jesus, earned the right to be there. Even the sinless Virgin Mary was redeemed by her Son.[94]

The Mercy and Justice of God

God's mercy does not contradict his justice, but "mercy triumphs over judgment" (Jas 2:13). God fulfills the demands of justice by sending his Son to die for us. As St. John Paul

II says: "At first sight judgment and mercy would seem to be two irreconcilable realities, or at least, the second seems to be connected with the first only if it mitigates its own inexorable power. It is necessary instead to understand the logic of sacred Scripture, which links them and indeed presents them in a way that one cannot exist without the other."[95] The judgment of God in the Old Testament is the way in which he expresses his mercy toward the oppressed. God is on a rescue mission, not on a power trip. As Jesus teaches us, "For God sent the Son into the world, not to condemn the world, but that the world might be saved through him" (Jn 3:17). While those who want to can reject him, Jesus offers salvation to all without exception and wills the salvation of all. Yet he can do so because he earned it. He paid for it with his blood. The power of his sacrifice is not limited to some arbitrary number, but is superabundant and available to everyone. God's power to have mercy on us is not illogical or inconsistent: "Nothing therefore can be in God's power which could not be in his just will or his wise intellect."[96] In his justice, God condemned sin on the cross. In his wisdom and mercy, he saved us through the Cross.

Teacher, Judge, Savior

Many of the troubles we have studied in the Bible are rooted in the imperfection and incompleteness of divine revelation before Jesus. As the great divine teacher, God slowly but surely reveals more and more of himself throughout the Old Testament. He uses the example of Israel to instruct us (1 Cor 10:11) about what it means to be faithful to God. The Old Testament stories in all of their enchanting complexity are meant to teach us, not just confuse us. In fact, the difficulty of the texts might be intentional, as St. Augustine argues. Perhaps God uses these texts to sharpen our minds, to get us thinking about his Word, and to motivate us to work through the challenges we find.

God the Judge plays a prominent role in the Bible, meting out justice and punishment regularly. The starkness of some of the judgments can shock us out of our chairs, but these events show the character of God. He is awesome in power, perfectly holy, and yet totally loving and infinitely merciful. Without a clear understanding of God's holiness, we don't understand how sinful sin is. Without an accurate perception of sin's evil, we wouldn't recognize our need for a Savior. God teaches us through his acts of justice how malignant the cancer of sin is and how much we should desire to be free from slavery to it. Only through that revelation can we appreciate the amazing gift of our redemption.

We are granted only a glimpse into eternity through Scripture, not the whole picture. Our knowledge in this life will always have that incomplete quality to it.

Jesus comes to deliver us. But from what? Some say Jesus comes to save us from a mean God, his Father. But that would look at the whole problem backward. Jesus comes to deliver us from a slavery, a bondage, to sin. Without him, we'll be stuck in a place of self-inflicted punishment, away from God's love and presence, trapped in our own conceit. Yet we don't have the power to deliver ourselves by our own best efforts. We desperately need a Savior to save us from our sins. Through his salvation, we are freed to live in "the glorious liberty of the children of God" (Rom 8:21). This newfound freedom is in accord with our nature as human beings. We were created to freely love, not to live in sinful selfishness.

Marvelous Mercy

The beauty of God's plan of salvation lies in its consistency. God is not arbitrary, shifting between strict exaction of justice and abundant mercy on a whim. Rather he has mercy on us through the justice of the Cross. He executes justice through the mercy of the Cross. His marvelous mercy comes to us as a free gift through his Son, but it was not free. We "were bought with a price" (1 Cor 6:20), the price of Christ's blood. The mercy of God is marvelous and abundant, available to "all who call upon him" (Rom 10:12). Jesus satisfies the requirements of God's justice on the cross and so offers us the reward purchased at a princely price.

His victory is complete. All we need to do is reach out and receive it. "Let us then with confidence draw near to the throne of grace, that we may receive mercy and find grace to help in time of need" (Heb 4:16).

Yet no matter how many times we return to the Word of God, we will not fully think it through in this life. There will always be more to discover, to analyze, to realize, and to come to appreciate. We are granted only a glimpse into eternity through Scripture, not the whole picture. Our knowledge in this life will always have that incomplete quality to it. Though it is incomplete, our view need not be inconsistent. We can find a way to fit the difficult, dark passages into a cohesive theological worldview. We can trust in both the mercy and the justice of God. We can rest in his victory while contemplating his complexity. If we give up that process of fitting the whole puzzle together, then we rob the Word of its power to challenge us, correct us, teach us, and reveal God to us.

The Bible is not just a collection of problems to be solved. It might confront us or make us squirm from time to time, but ultimately it points to our destiny. After judgment, after mercy, after repentance, after redemption, we long for something far greater than our earthly existence. We long to be one with God, to have our whole being filled with his presence, to see him face to face.

We can trust not only in the truth of the Word, but in the justice and mercy of God, who invites us to that eternal union with him. He is the God who sees himself as a loving groom, beckoning his bride: "And I will betroth you to me for ever; I will betroth you to me in righteousness and in justice, in steadfast love, and in mercy" (Hos 2:19).

Though our curiosity will always long for more intellectual satisfaction, God offers us the better part, to be one with him forever in both justice *and* mercy. Perhaps the "dark passages" have a way of leading us back to the Light after all.

1 *Catechism of the Catholic Church*, second ed. (Washington: United States Catholic Conference, 1997), 109-114. Henceforth, *CCC*.

2 St. Thomas Aquinas, *Summa Theologica* I, q. 1, a. 10. The Pontifical Biblical Commission (*Interpretation of the Bible in the Church*, II.B.2) refers to the literal sense as the "indispensable foundation" of spiritual interpretation.

3 For a recent academic treatment from a Catholic theological perspective, see Matthew Ramage, *The Dark Passages of the Bible: Engaging Scripture with Benedict XVI and Thomas Aquinas* (Washington, DC: The Catholic University of America Press, 2013).

4 Benedict XVI, *Verbum Domini*, September 30, 2010, 42. http://www.vatican.va/holy_father/benedict_xvi/apost_exhortations/documents/hf_ben-xvi_exh_20100930_verbum-domini_en.html.

5 Ibid.

6 *City of God*, 11.19. *De Genesi ad litteram*, 21.19.

7 Patrick Burke, "Illinois Spent $2.26M on Cable TV for Prisons," *CNS News*, December 5, 2012, http://cnsnews.com/news/article/illinois-spent-226m-cable-tv-prisons.

8 See *CCC*, 2267.

9 See Gn 12:18; 26:10; 29:25.

10 See *CCC*, 403-406.

11 *CCC*, 1008.

12 Alexia D. Cooper, Matthew R. Durose, Howard N. Synder, "Recidivism of Prisoners Released in 30 States in 2005: Patterns from 2005 to 2010," April 22, 2014, http://www.bjs.gov/index.cfm?ty=pbdetail&iid=4987.

13 For example, see Ps 9:7; 11:4; 93:1; Is 6:1; Rv 4:1-11.

14 Also in Absalom's coup in 2 Samuel 15:1-6. Although the ancient Israelite king was executive and judge, it is not clear that he had a legislative role.

15 For a scholarly study on the judicial role of the ancient Israelite king, see Keith Whitelam, *The Just King: Monarchial Judicial Authority in Ancient Israel*, JSOTSup 12 (Sheffield, UK: JSOT Press, 1979).

16 See Rom 2:6; 1 Pt 1:17; Rv 2:2,19,23; 3:1,8,15.

17 Suetonius, *Lives of the Caesars*, "Claudius," 14-15, http://penelope.uchicago.edu/Thayer/E/Roman/Texts/Suetonius/12Caesars/Claudius*.html.

18 Jerome, *Live of Illustrious Men*, NPNF2, vol. 3, chap. 5., http://www.ccel.org/ccel/schaff/npnf203.v.iii.vii.html.

19 Eusebius, *Ecclesiastical History*, II.25, http://www.newadvent.org/fathers/250102.htm.

20 See 2 Sm 11:3; 16:20-21; 23:34.

21 The embarrassment of everyone knowing what was happening in the rooftop tent might seem like punishment enough to us, but in biblical times marriages were consummated in a semi-public way in a bridal chamber or tent (Ps 19:5; Jl 2:16) immediately following the public wedding ceremony—a practice referred to as *yichud*, "togetherness." See Blu Greenberg, "Marriage in the Jewish Tradition," *Journal of Ecumenical Studies* 22 (1985):3-20, here 11.

22 *CCC*, 53.

23 John Paul II, "The Spirit of Faith Is Essential to Every Christian Catechesis," General Audience, January 16, 1985, http://www.vatican.va/holy_father/john_paul_ii/audiences/alpha/data/aud19850116en.html.

24 Vatican II, *Dei Verbum*, 12, http://www.vatican.va/archive/hist_councils/ii_vatican_council/documents/vat-ii_const_19651118_dei-verbum_en.html.

25 *CCC*, 708.

26 See *Summa Theologica*, I-II, q. 99.

27 *CCC*, 65.

28 For example, see John Paul II, *Evangelium vitae* (1995), 56, http://www.vatican.va/holy_father/john_paul_ii/encyclicals/documents/hf_jp-ii_enc_25031995_evangelium-vitae_en.html.

29 Gn 6:5-17; 19:24-25; Ex 12:29; Nm 16:35; plagues: Ex 32:35; Nm 11:33, 16:49; 25:9; 2 Sm 24:15.

30 Gn 19:26; 38:7; 38:9-10; Lv 10:1; 1 Kgs 20:36; Acts 5:1-10; 12:23.

31 For example, see Is 57:7-8; Ez 6:9; Hos 4:10-14; 1 Cor 6:9.

32 *CCC*, 2263-65.

33 *CCC*, 2267.

34 *CCC*, 2309.

35 This Hebrew term comes from the verb *charam*, to "exterminate, utterly destroy."

36 Library of Congress, "History of the American West, 1860-1920," http://www.lcweb.loc.gov/teachers/classroommaterials/connections/hist-am-west/history.html.

37 Richard Hess ("The Jericho and Ai of the Book of Joshua," *Critical Issues in the Early Israelite History*, eds. Richard Hess, Gerard Klingbeil, and Paul Ray [Winona Lake, IN: Eisenbrauns, 2008], 33-46, here 35); cites 2 Sm 5:7,9; 12:26; and 1 Chr 11:5,7 to argue, "The evidence suggests that *'îr* can at times designate what is primarily a fort."

38 John Day, "Canaan, Religion of," *Anchor Bible Dictionary*, vol. 1, 831-37, here 835.

39 See Jos 8:25; 1 Sm 22:19; 1 Chr 16:3; Neh 8:2.

40 Hess, "Jericho and Ai," 45.

41 Ibid., 46.

42 Paul Jeffrey, "Civilian Militias Defend Sudanese Villages from Rebel Army Attacks," *Catholic News Service*, http://www.catholicnews.com/data/stories/cns/1004954.htm.

43 This figure shows up elsewhere: Is 47:1; Jer 50:42; 51:33; Zec 2:7.

44 See Hess, "Jericho and Ai," 39.

45 *CCC*, 1283.

46 See Diodorus Siculus, *Library*, XX, xiv.

47 See David Schloen, *The House of the Father as Fact and Symbol: Patrimonialism in Ugarit and the Ancient Near East* (Winona Lake, IN: Eisenbrauns, 2001), 138.

48 *CCC*, 1037.

49 See *CCC*, 400.

50 John Paul II, *Salvifici Doloris*, 11, http://w2.vatican.va/content/john-paul-ii/en/apost_letters/1984/documents/hf_jp-ii_apl_11021984_salvifici-doloris.html.

51 See *CCC*, 1008.

52 John Paul II (*Salvifici Doloris*, 31) writes, "The mystery of the Redemption of the world is in an amazing way *rooted in suffering*, and this suffering finds in the mystery of the Redemption its supreme and surest point of reference."

53 Michal (1 Sm 18:27); Ahinoam and Abigail (1 Sm 25:43); Maacah, Haggith, Abital, and Eglah (2 Sm 3:5); Bathsheba (2 Sm 11:27).

54 Genesis 25:1 reports that Abraham married Keturah, but it is not clear whether this took place before or after Sarah's death.

55 Genesis 25:6 mentions Abraham's "concubines," but Hagar is the only one named in Genesis.

56 St. Augustine, *On Marriage and Concupiscence*, in vol. 5, *Anti-Pelagian Writings*, of *The Nicene and Post-Nicene Fathers*, Series I, edited by Philip Schaff, repr. ed. (Peabody, MA: Hendrickson, 1994), I.10.

57 John Paul II, *Familiaris Consortio*, November 11, 1981, 19, http://www.vatican.va/holy_father/john_paul_ii/apost_exhortations/documents/hf_jp-ii_exh_19811122_familiaris-consortio_en.html.

58 St. Augustine affirms the unity of the human family in this way: "We may note that racial differences affect external characteristics only. The essential agreement of all races in physical structure and in mental endowment indicates a common origin." *In Ioan.* tr. 9, 10.

59 *Code of Canon Law*, 1091-94.

60 *CCC*, 2383.

61 *CCC*, 2384.

62 *CCC*, 2414.

63 Dante, *Inferno*, Canto III, line 6.

64 *CCC*, 1033.

65   Benedict XVI, *Spe Salvi*, November 30, 2007, 45, http://www.vatican.va/holy_father/benedict_xvi/encyclicals/documents/hf_ben-xvi_enc_20071130_spe-salvi_en.html.

66   See, for example, International Theological Commission, "The Hope of Salvation for Infants Who Die Without Being Baptised," http://www.vatican.va/roman_curia/congregations/cfaith/cti_documents/rc_con_cfaith_doc_20070419_un-baptised-infants_en.html.

67   *CCC*, 1261.

68   J. Neuner and J. Dupuis, *The Christian Faith in the Doctrinal Documents of the Catholic Church*, 7th ed. (New York: Alba House, 2001), 26.

69   *Summa Theologica* Suppl., q. 94, a. 3.

70   *CCC*, 121.

71   St. Thomas Aquinas, *Summa Theologica*, 2nd, rev. ed., trans. Fathers of the English Dominican Province (1920; New Advent, 2008): I-II, q. 98, a. 1, http://newadvent.org/summa/2098.htm.

72   Vatican II, *Dei Verbum*, 15, http://www.vatican.va/archive/hist_councils/ii_vatican_council/documents/vat-ii_const_19651118_dei-verbum_en.html.

73   *Summa Theologica*, I, q. 70, a. 1, ad. 3.

74   Leo XIII, *Providentissimus Deus*, November 18, 1893, 18, http://www.vatican.va/holy_father/leo_xiii/encyclicals/documents/hf_l-xiii_enc_18111893_providentissimus-deus_en.html.

75   Pius XI, *Mit Brennender Sorge*, March 14, 1937, 15, http://www.vatican.va/holy_father/pius_xi/encyclicals/documents/hf_p-xi_enc_14031937_mit-brennender-sorge_en.html.

76   Pontifical Biblical Commission, *Interpretation of the Bible in the Church*, April 15, 1993, §I, F.

77   Pius XI, *Mit Brennender Sorge*, 15.

78   *De Doctrina Christiana*, Book I, chap. 36, http://www.ccel.org/ccel/augustine/doctrine.xxxvi.html.

79   *CCC*, 122, quoting *Dei Verbum*, 15.

80   John Paul II, *Catechesi Tradendae*, October 16, 1979, 58, http://www.vatican.va/holy_father/john_paul_ii/apost_exhortations/documents/hf_jp-ii_exh_16101979_catechesi-tradendae_en.html.

81   *CCC*, 1008.

82   Of course, we must also be on guard against a literalism that does violence to the meaning of the text by disregarding its historical origins or its literary form.

83   *Rule of St. Benedict*, chapter 73, http://www.osb.org/lectio/rbonld.html.

84   *CCC*, 1008.

85   *CCC*, 616.

86   *CCC*, 605.

87   Like "homicide" means man-killing, "deicide" means god-killing.

88   *Summa Theologica*, III, q. 46, a. 2.

89   St. Anselm speculates on this point that the satisfaction must be proportional to the offense, so our sin is an infinite offense against God, demanding an infinite satisfaction, which only the God-man, Jesus, could provide.

90   See *CCC*, 1991-92.

91   John Paul II, *Salvifici Doloris*, February 11, 1984, 30, http://www.vatican.va/holy_father/john_paul_ii/apost_letters/1984/documents/hf_jp-ii_apl_11021984_salvifici-doloris_en.html.

92   St. Augustine, *City of God*, 11.19, http://www.newadvent.org/fathers/120111.htm.

93   *CCC*, 1011.

94   *CCC*, 492.

95   John Paul II, *General Audience*, July 7, 1999, 1, http://www.vatican.va/holy_father/john_paul_ii/audiences/1999/documents/hf_jp-ii_aud_07071999_en.html.

96   *Summa Theologica* I, q. 25, a. 5, quoted in *CCC*, 271.

ABOUT THE AUTHOR

Mark Giszczak holds a Ph.D. in biblical studies from the Catholic University of America and is Associate Professor of Sacred Scripture at the Augustine Institute in Colorado. He writes often at CatholicExchange.com and his blog, CatholicBibleStudent.com. Through his writing, teaching and speaking, he loves to help Catholics read, study, and pray the Bible. Mark lives in Denver, Colorado with his wife and children.